WHERE'S ELVIS?
and many others...

Illustrations **Daniel Lalic**
Text **Xavier Waterkeyn**

NEW HOLLAND

Dedication
Daniel dedicates his illustrations to:
Edo Lalic 1925–1995
Boris Grbic 1927-2008

Xavier dedicates his words and ideas to:
Guy Waterkeyn 1925-1985
Marcella Waterkeyn
Tony Esposito, Jacqui Waterkeyn, Sebastian and Stefan

To everyone out there who never wants the music to die

Acknowledgements
Daniel and Xavier would like to thank each other for being
there as well as the team at New Holland for their work especially,
Lliane Clarke for overseeing things, Hayley Norman for her
design work and Fiona Schultz for giving us another
opportunity to slaughter a few sacred cows.

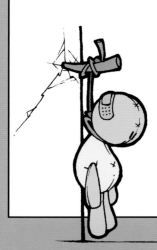

Officials are still investigating the mysterious bombing of the headquarters of Viva! Magazine in downtown Memphis Tennessee on New Year's Day 2010. A few days later a large brown paper envelope mysteriously appeared in our offices. None of the staff could attest to how it came to be there. When we opened it we discovered a group of 12 panoramic photographs and accompanying notes, which, if authentic, hold staggering implications.

Accompanying the photographs was a letter, somewhat singed and smoke-damaged. You will note that the letter is incomplete, but the facsimile of the document is reproduced on the following page as we received it.

Our investigations have revealed that it purports to be confidential correspondence between Ernie Lovejoy, photo researcher for Viva! Magazine, and his Editor-In-Chief, Samantha Packenpen. The originals are currently under forensic examination. We cannot at this time vouch for the authenticity of the letter or the photographs but we feel it is in the public interest to be informed of what may be one of the greatest hoaxes and conspiracies ever perpetrated on the unsuspecting masses.

We believe that the dissemination of these facts, presented to you now, is especially important, given that, as at the time of writing, both Ernie Lovejoy and Samantha Packenpen have completely vanished without a trace.

–Memphis Bugle Jan 10, 2010

For Your Eyes Only!!!

Sammy,

Sorry for all the secrecy up till now and I know you'll think I'm crazy but hear me out. I have to write this because I think my phone is being bugged and I can't risk anyone finding anything on my hard drive.

Remember when you asked me to start collecting images for our special January 10, 2010 issue 'Elvis – A Platinum Jubilee Retrospective'??? Well, it all started when I accidently found a rare shot of the man taken during the wrap up party on the set of 'Jailhouse Rock'. When I examined the picture closely I found something. I couldn't believe it! There in the crowd of the party was James Dean. I didn't even know that they knew each other, but then I looked at the date of the photo. Jimmy Dean was already dead when the photo was taken!!! I thought it had to be a fake. But I couldn't imagine why anyone would fake this. I can't go into details now, but I eventually found an informant who provided me with other shots. Sammy, the photos span decades and they all show people who were supposedly dead at the time the photo was taken or who died shortly after. Nearly all of them died young. Another pattern that I discerned was the fact that many, but not all, of these 'dead' people had since become even more famous in death than in life. Some of them even made more money after they died than while they were alive!!!

You can imagine my shock when I was shown photos taken even after Elvis' death, all of which show him hidden somewhere in the shot. You always have to look hard to find him.

What did this all mean? My informant refused to say and wanted me to work it out for myself. I came up with a theory, and when I confronted my informant about it they didn't deny it!!! Elvis was actually behind an amazingly daring plan to fake the deaths of his celebrity friends. Why? So that they could really cash in on post-mortem cult followings, get political mileage out of becoming martyrs or at the very least avoid annoying fans, complicated private lives, legal troubles or the tax man – in short, problems that were building up and making their lives impossible. Most suspicious of all is that even after his supposed 'death' Elvis continued to not only reap the benefits of his own master plan, but continued to recruit more celebrities to what I think of as his 'secret club of pseudo death'. Look Sammy, I don't expect you just to take my word for it. Look at the enclosed twelve images. Find Elvis hiding in the

DEAD STARS
ELVIS
MONROE
JAMES DEAN
BUDDY HOLLY
J.P.
RITCHIE VALENS
MARLEY
JIM HENDRIX
JOPLIN
BRIAN
KING
JOHN LENNON
CHE GUEVARA

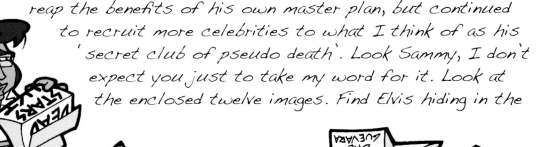

crowds! Find the people who have faked their way from ordinary stardom to superstardom or even to icon status! And check out the ones whose 'after death' expectations didn't lead to the 'afterlife' cash-in they were expecting! Check out the other stuff too. Each photo has several recurring objects in them that seem to follow Elvis everywhere he goes: 1) A HAMBURGER, 2) a PAIR OF BLUE SUEDE SHOES, 3) a TCB BLACK BELT, 4) a HOUND DOG, 5) there's this guy I've called 'MOONIE' with blue painted buttocks who keeps flashing his backside to the camera (I don't know what the hell he's doing there or what it means), 6) a TEDDY BEAR, 7) a GOLD RECORD, 8) what looks like the G.I. ISSUE UNDERPANTS that Elvis wore when he was in the army and his 9) DOG TAGS. I've also provided a list of notes of the people I've managed to identify, Sammy. See if you can spot them too and tell me that I'm not imagining all this!!!!! One picture even contains a gold key to a Cadillac. Sammy, I've got to go and send this off to you. Remember that each picture contains:

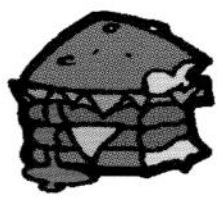
A hamburger

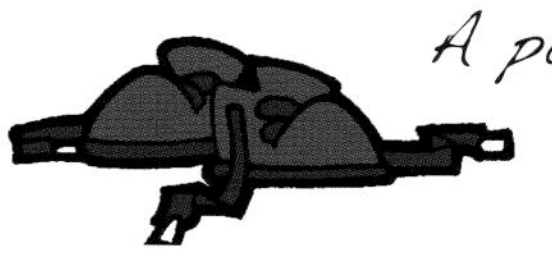
A pair of blue suede shoes

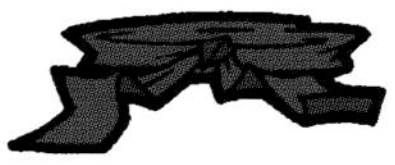
A TCB black belt

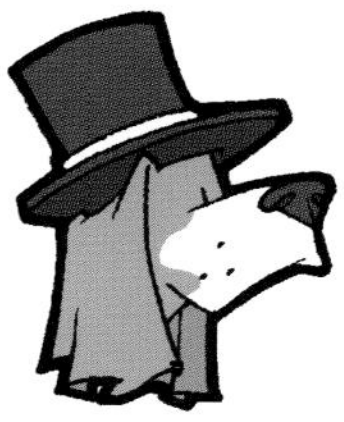
A hound dog

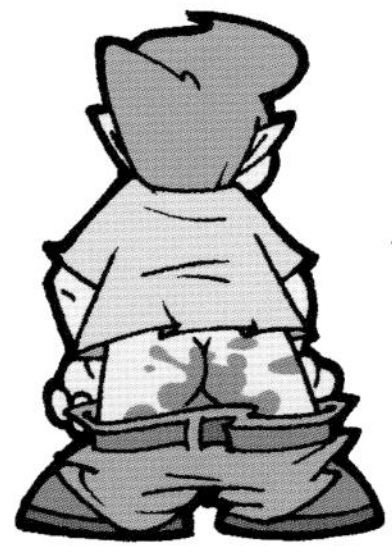
That guy with blue painted buttocks who keeps flashing his backside to the camera

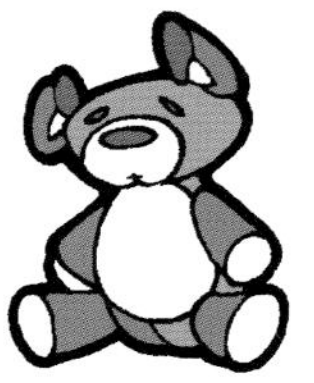
A teddy bear

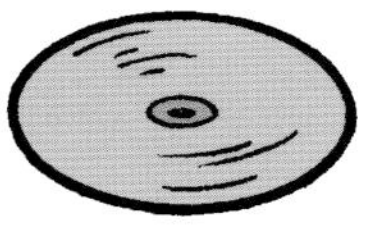
A gold record

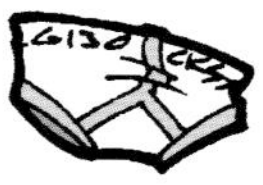
G.I. issue underpants

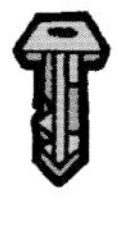
One picture contains a gold key

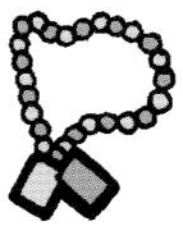
Dog tags

Yours,

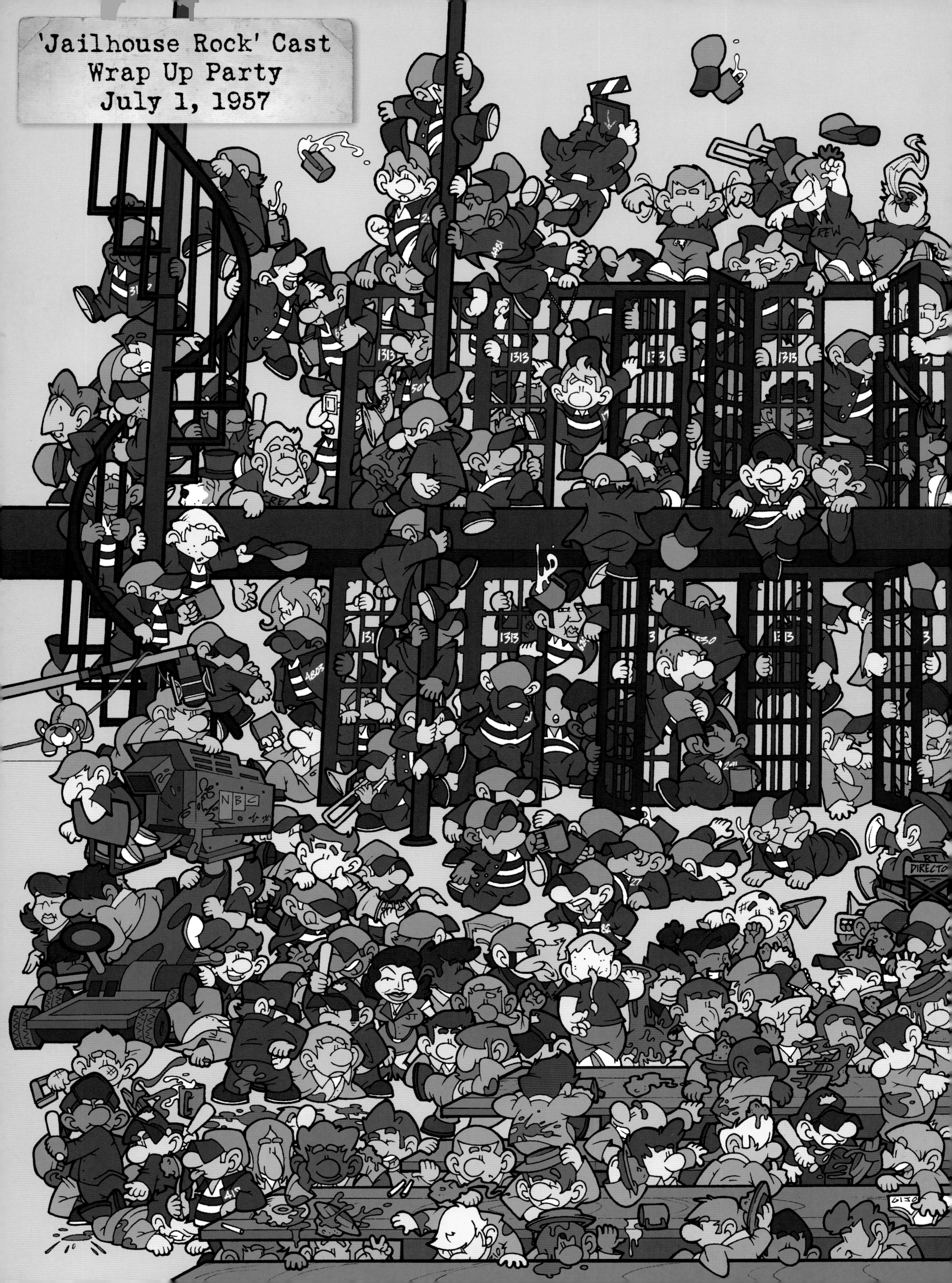
'Jailhouse Rock' Cast
Wrap Up Party
July 1, 1957
NBC
1313

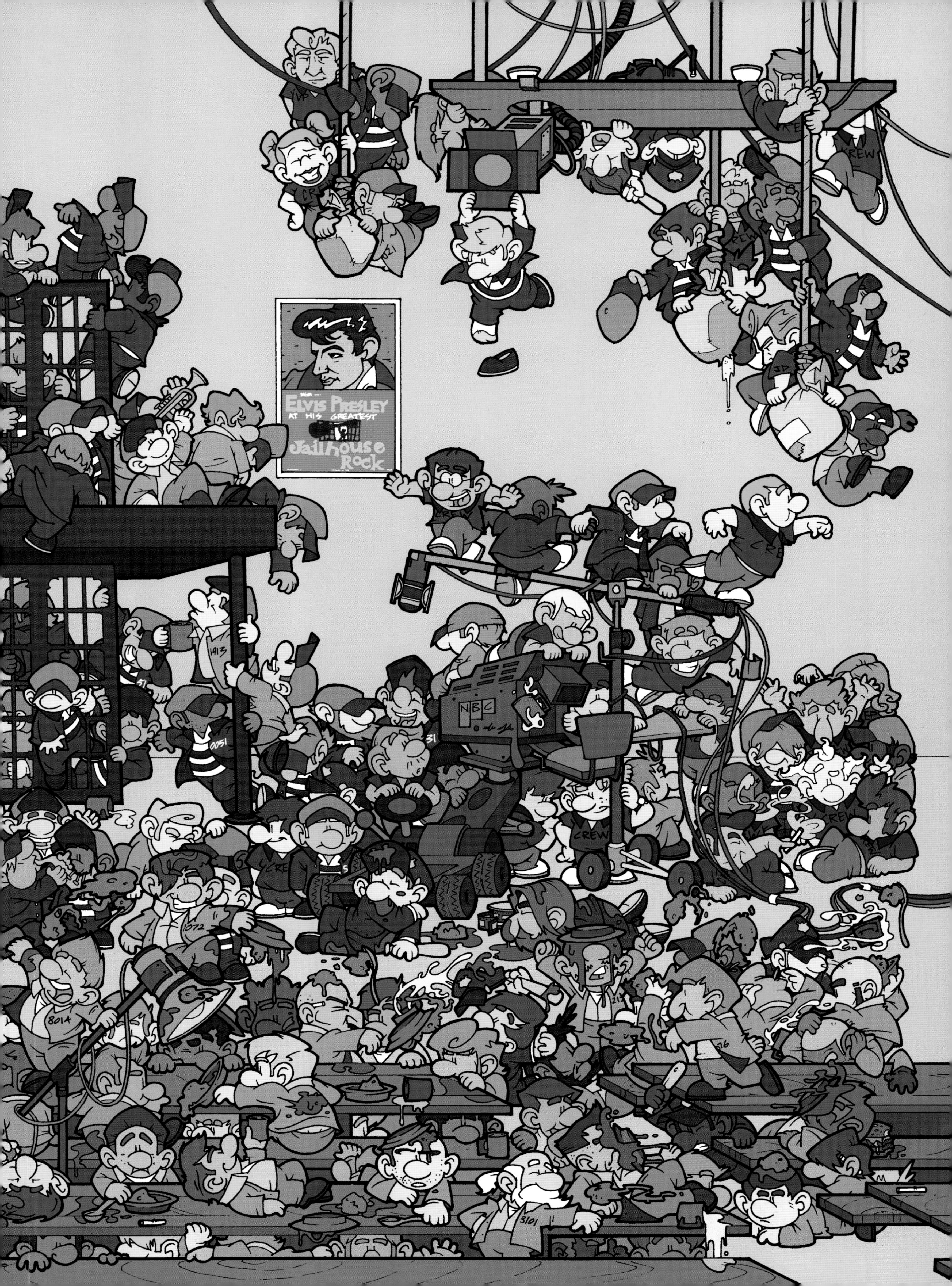
ELVIS PRESLEY
AT HIS GREATEST
Jailhouse Rock
NBC
CREW
1913
0051
31
1072
8014
3101

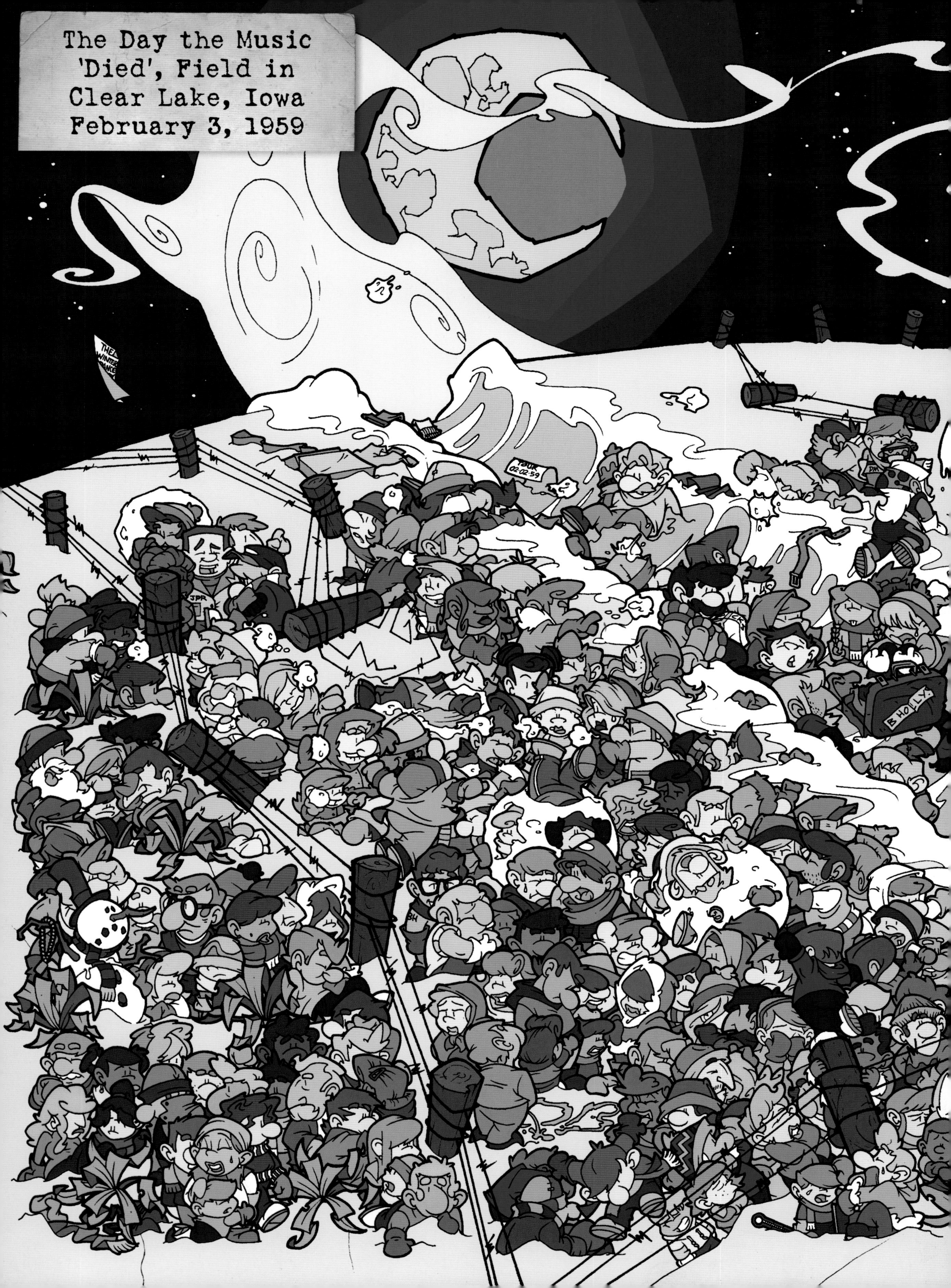
The Day the Music 'Died', Field in Clear Lake, Iowa February 3, 1959
TOUR 02·02·59
JPR
B HOLLY

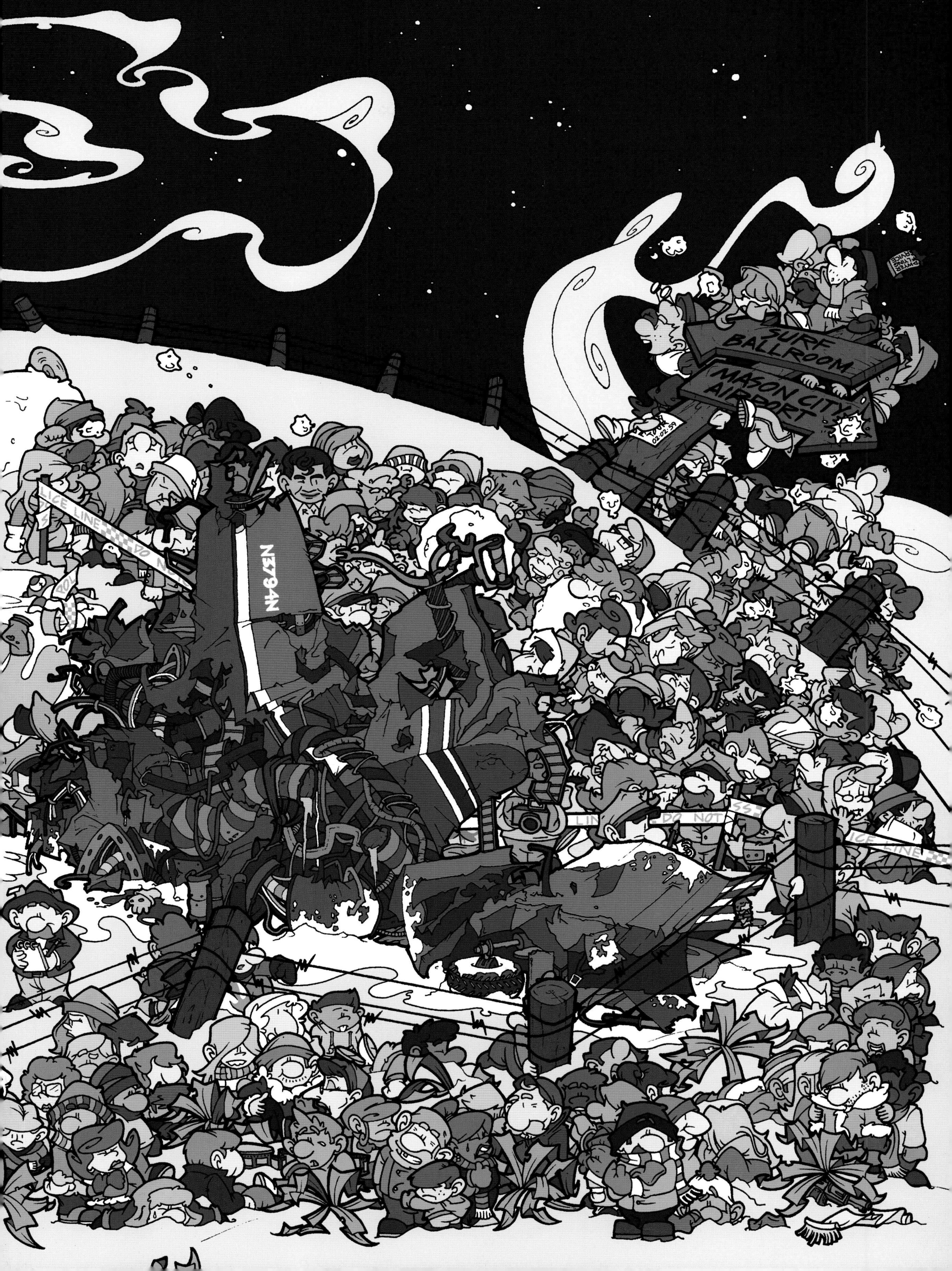
SURF BALLROOM
MASON CITY AIRPORT
02.02.59
N3794N
DO NOT

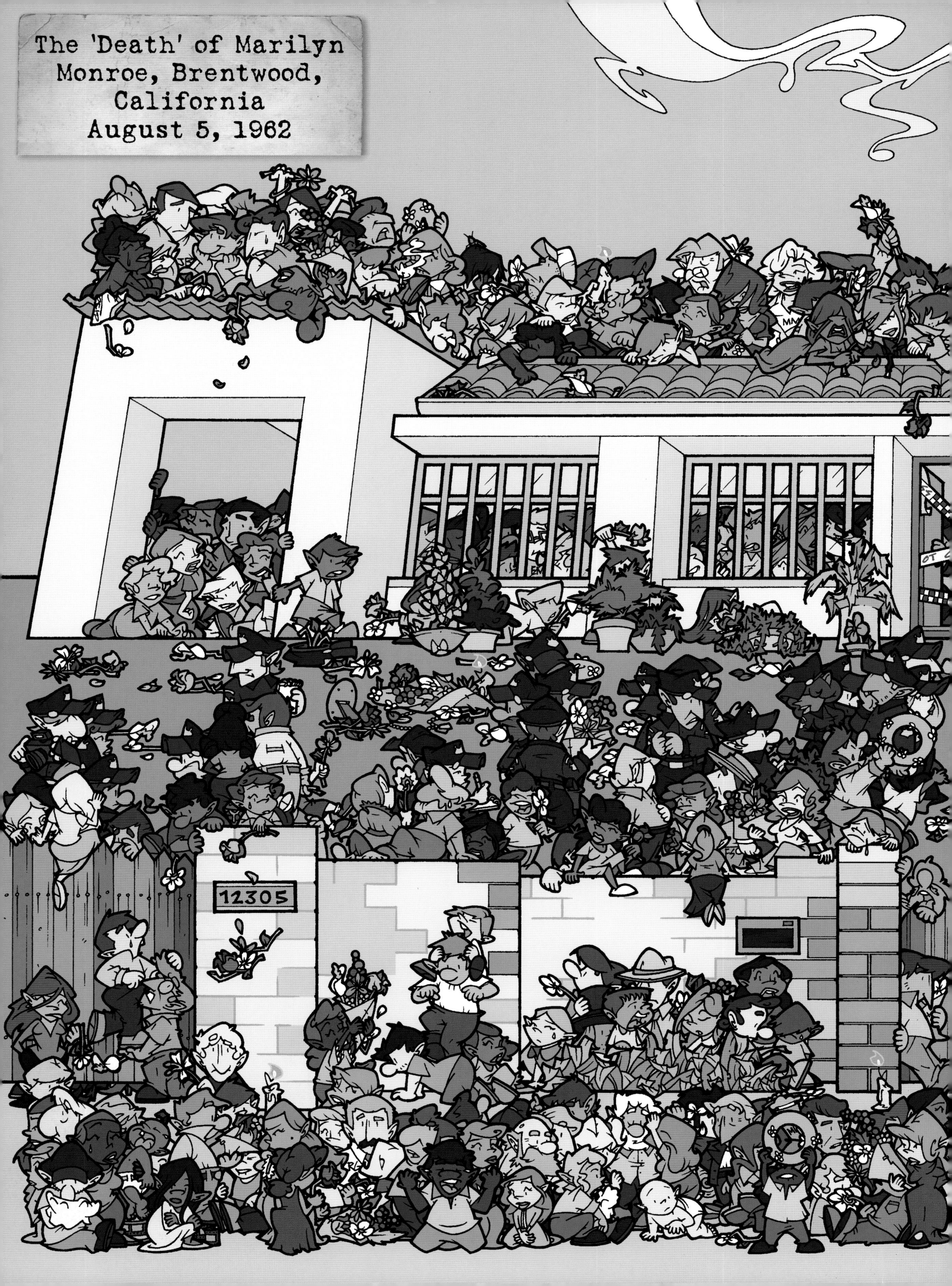
12305

The 'Death' of Marilyn Monroe, Brentwood, California August 5, 1962

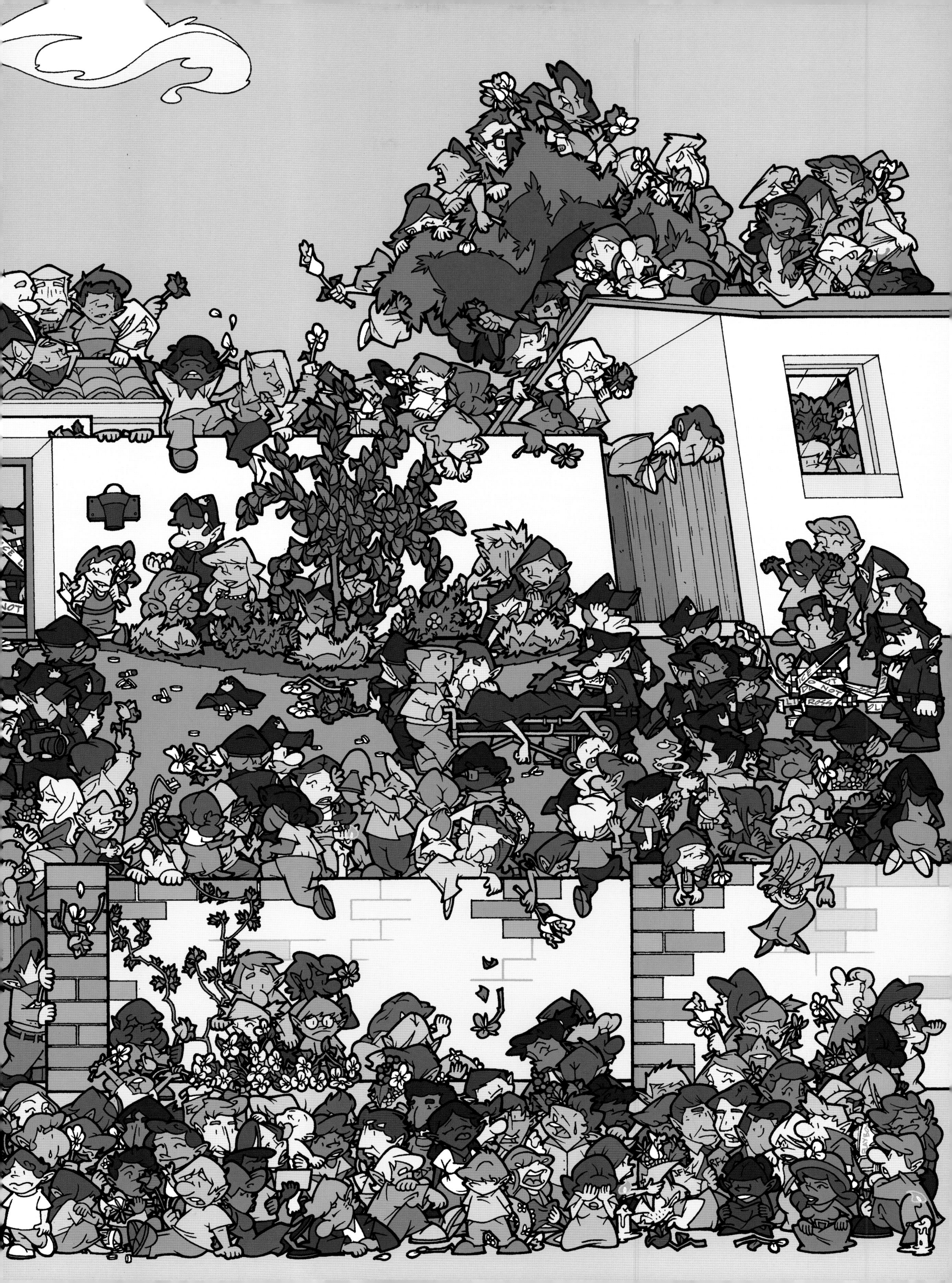
DO NOT
ROSS

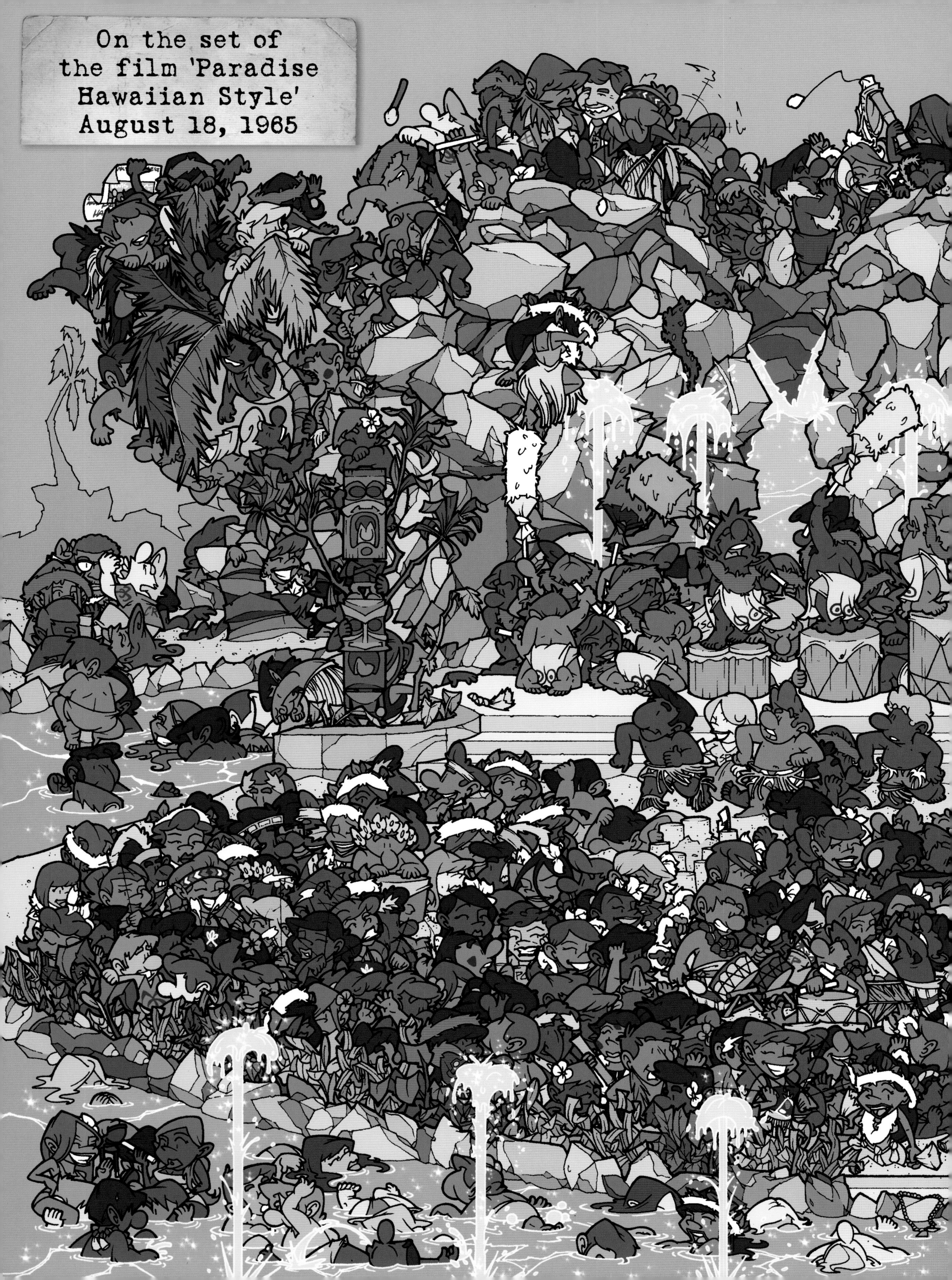
On the set of
the film 'Paradise
Hawaiian Style'
August 18, 1965

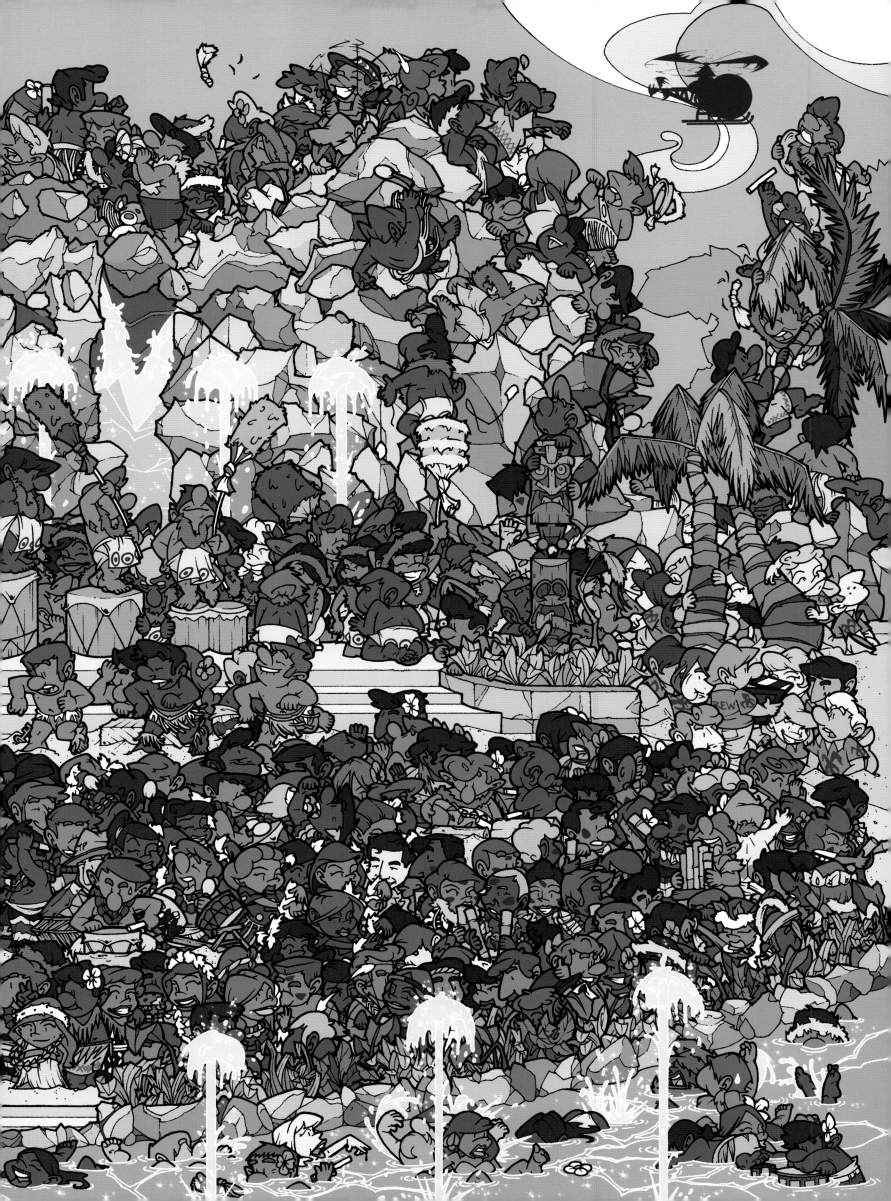

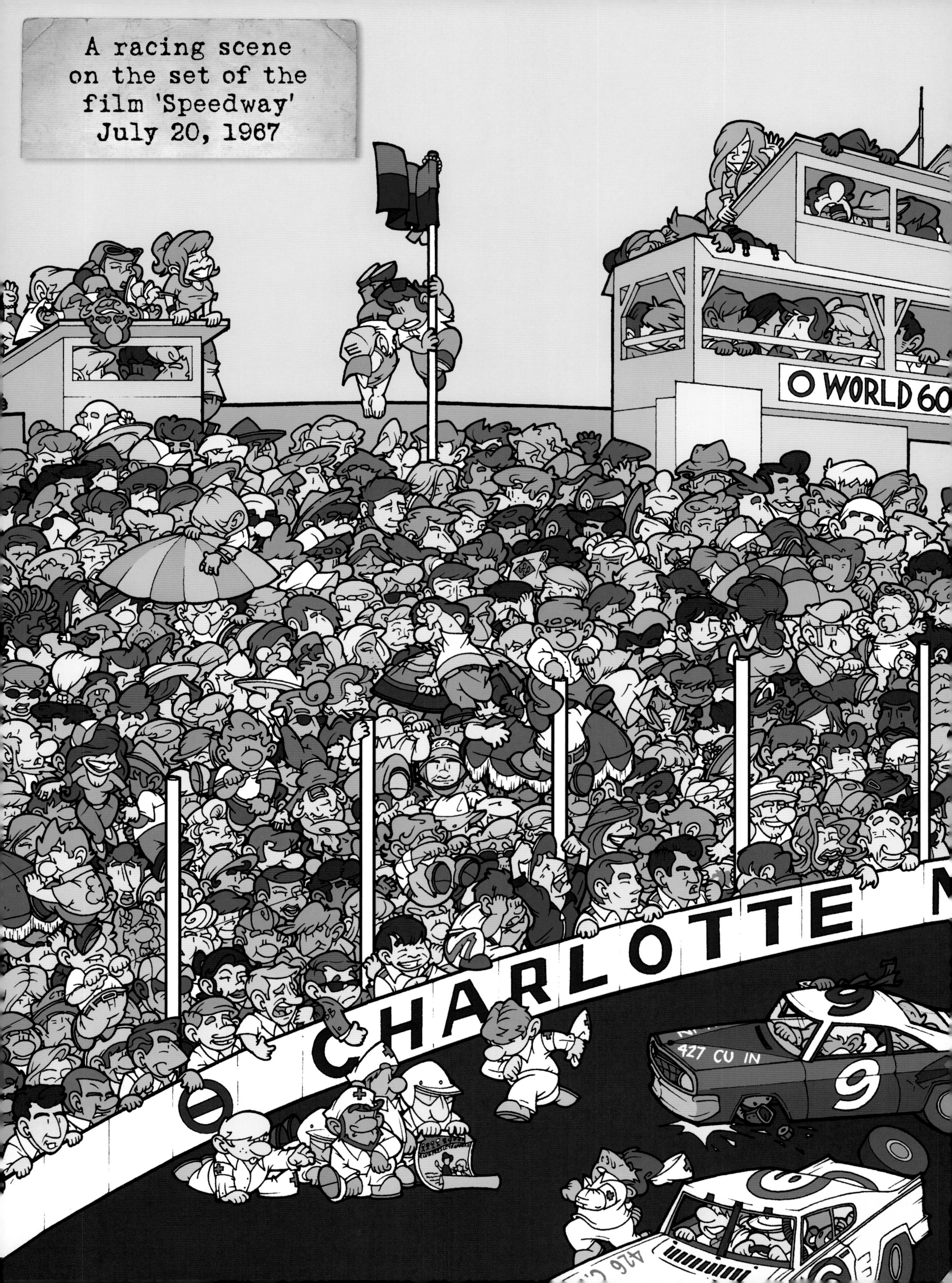
A racing scene on the set of the film 'Speedway' July 20, 1967
WORLD 60
CHARLOTTE
427 CU IN
9

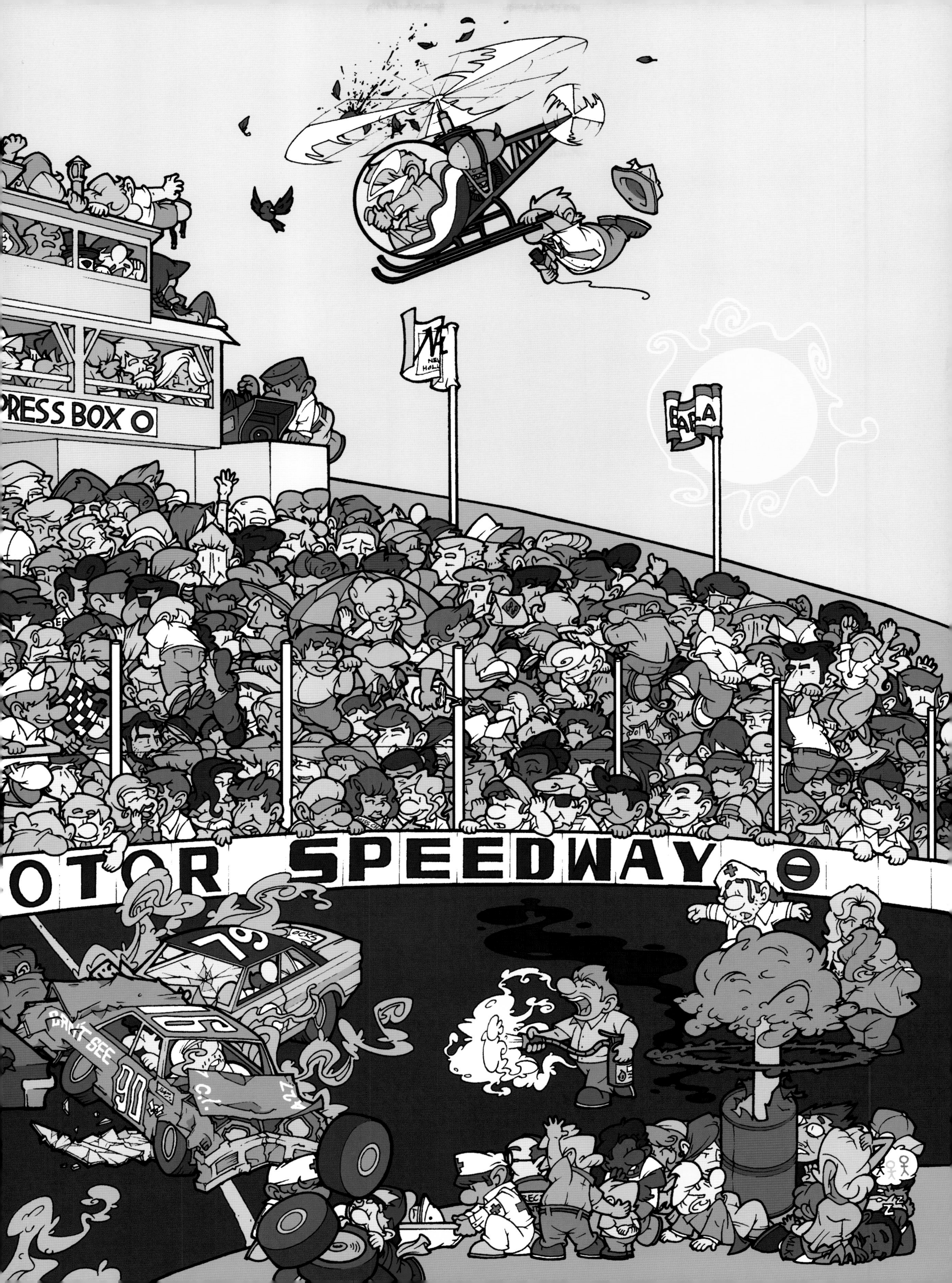
PRESS BOX
OTOR SPEEDWAY
79
90

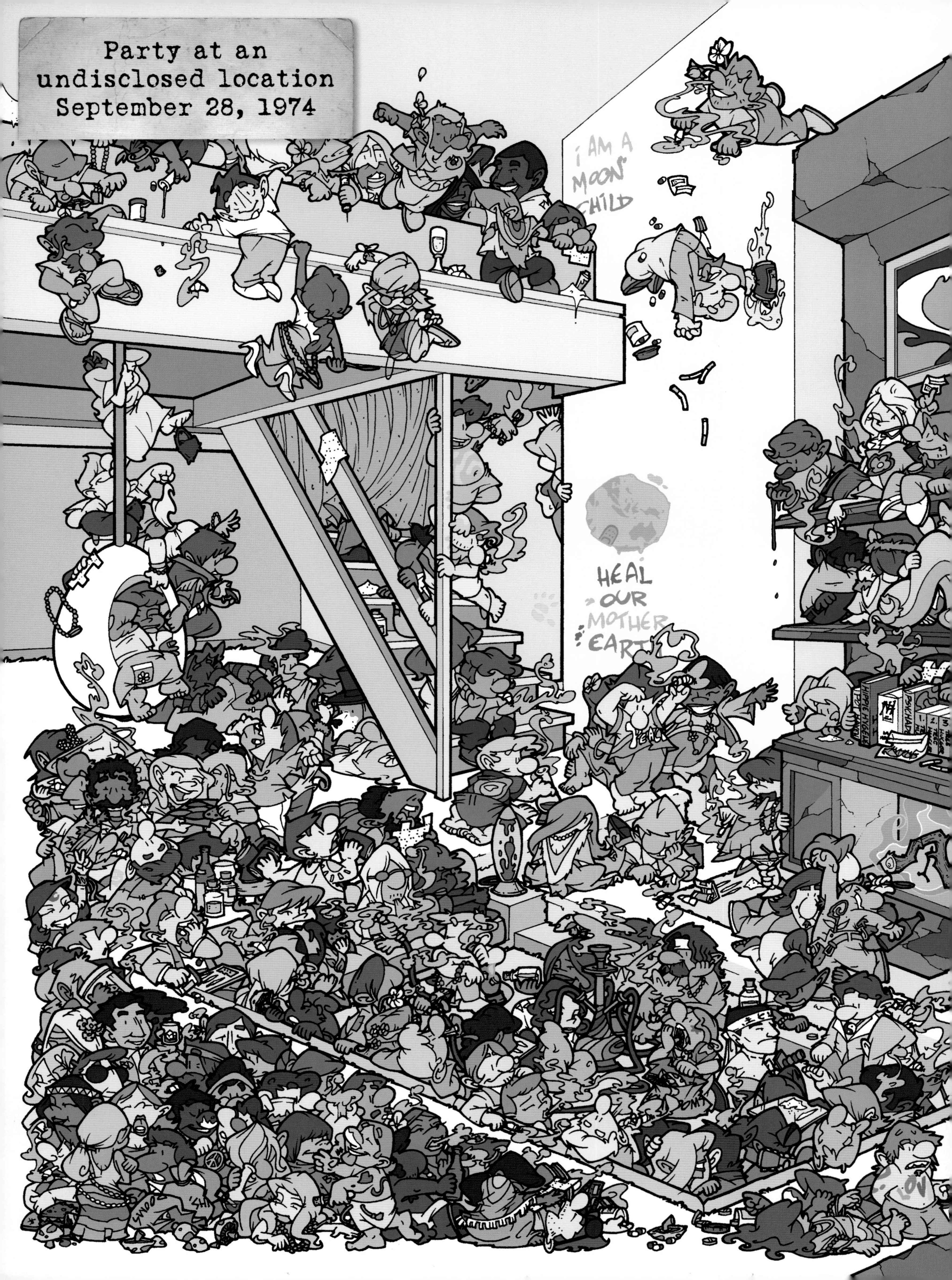
Party at an
undisclosed location
September 28, 1974
I AM A MOON CHILD
HEAL OUR MOTHER EART

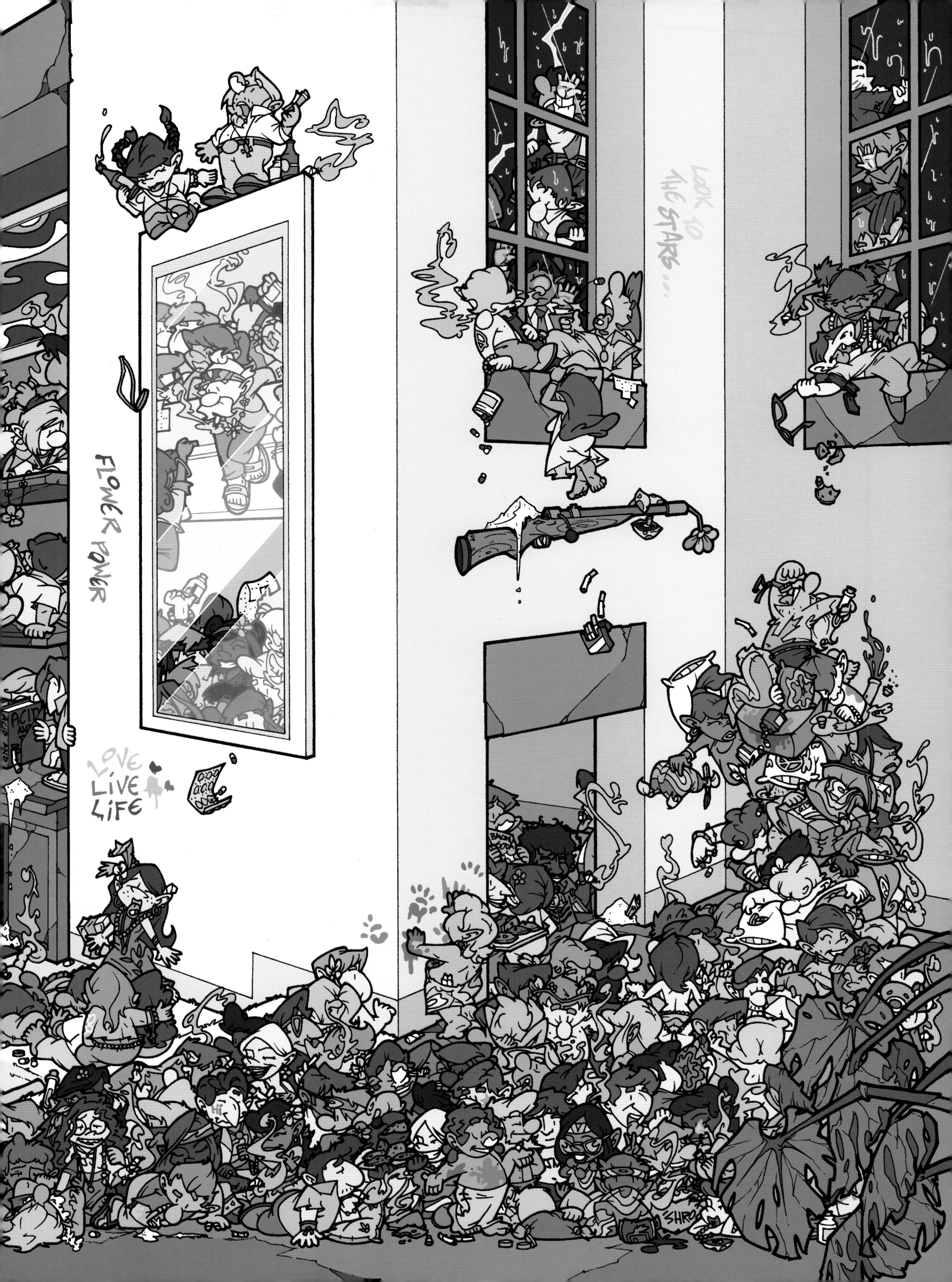
LOOK TO THE STARS...
FLOWER POWER
LOVE LIVE LIFE

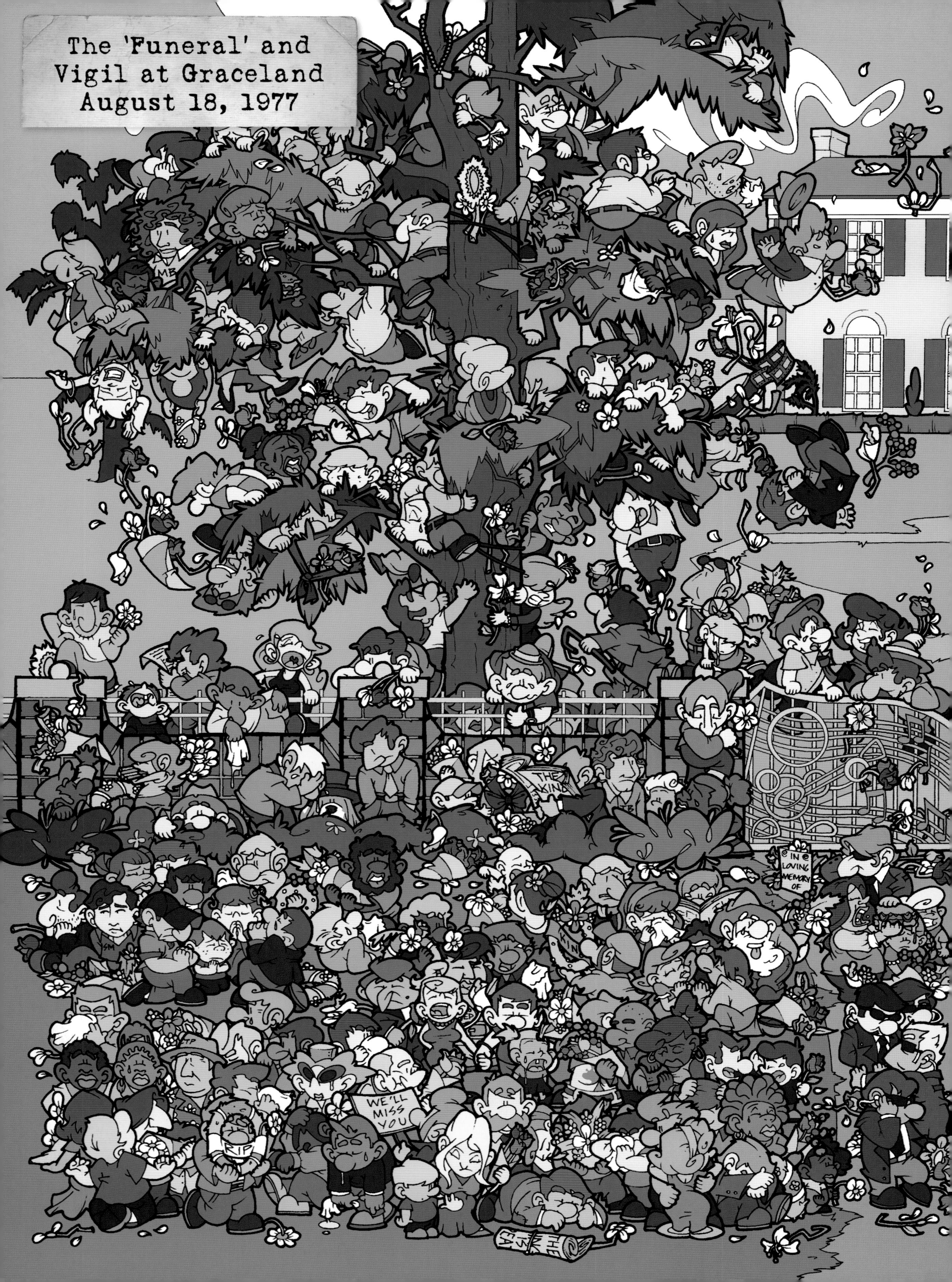
THE KING
IN LOVING MEMORY OF
WE'LL MISS YOU
The 'Funeral' and Vigil at Graceland August 18, 1977

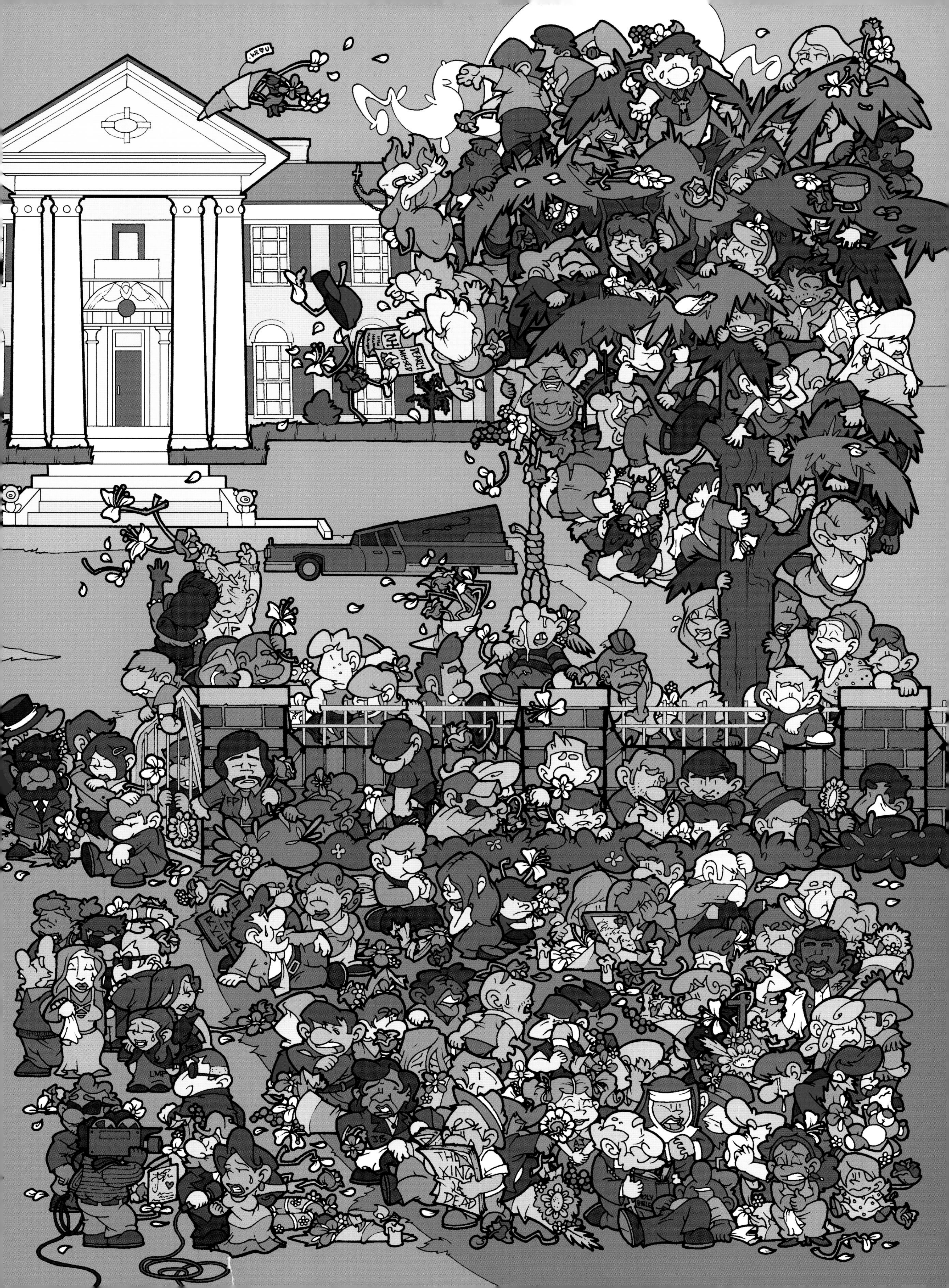
WE ♥ U
NH
DEARLY MISSED
VP
FP
LMP
JB
THE KING IS DEAD
HOLY BIBLE

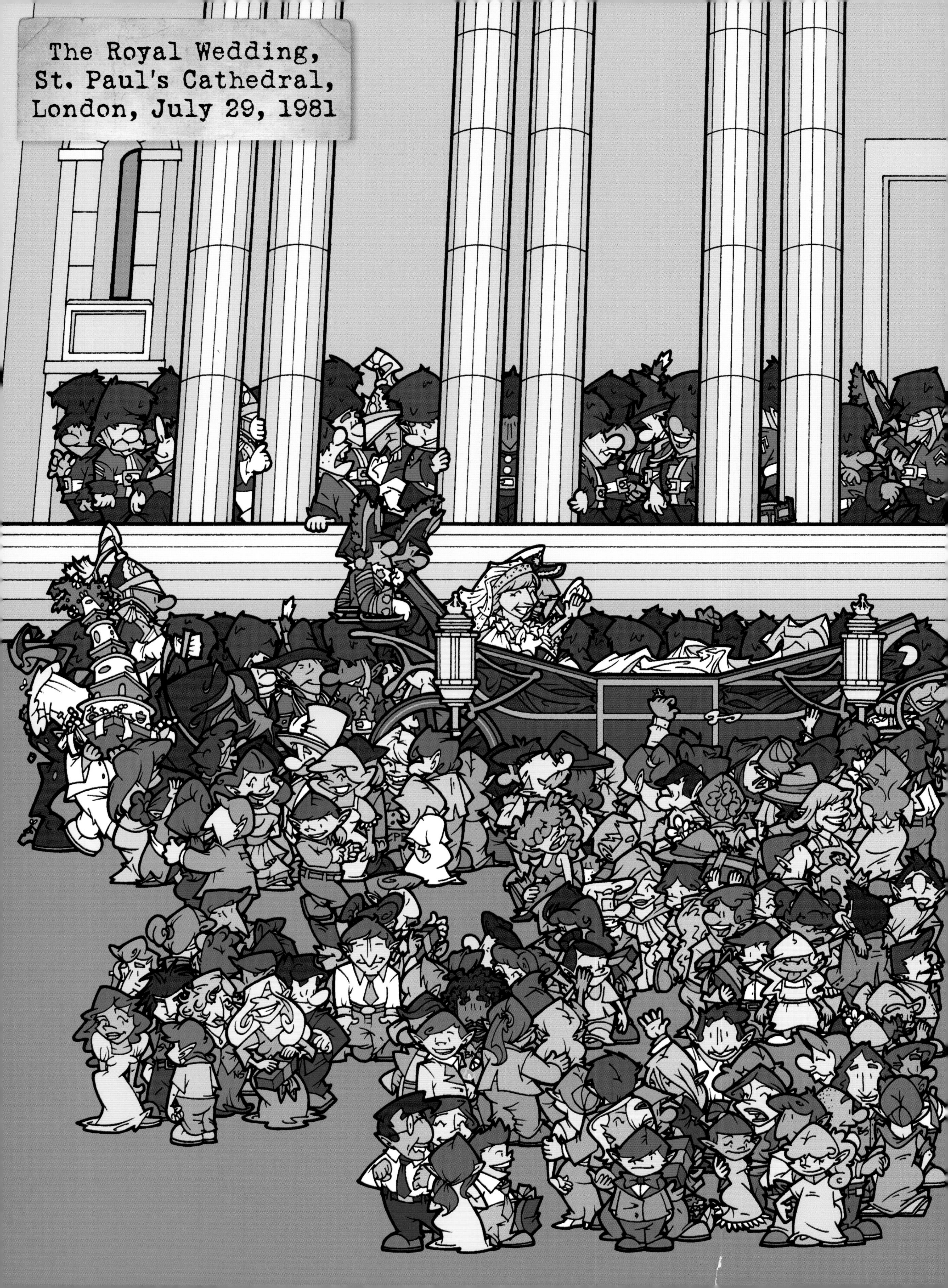

The Royal Wedding,
St. Paul's Cathedral,
London, July 29, 1981

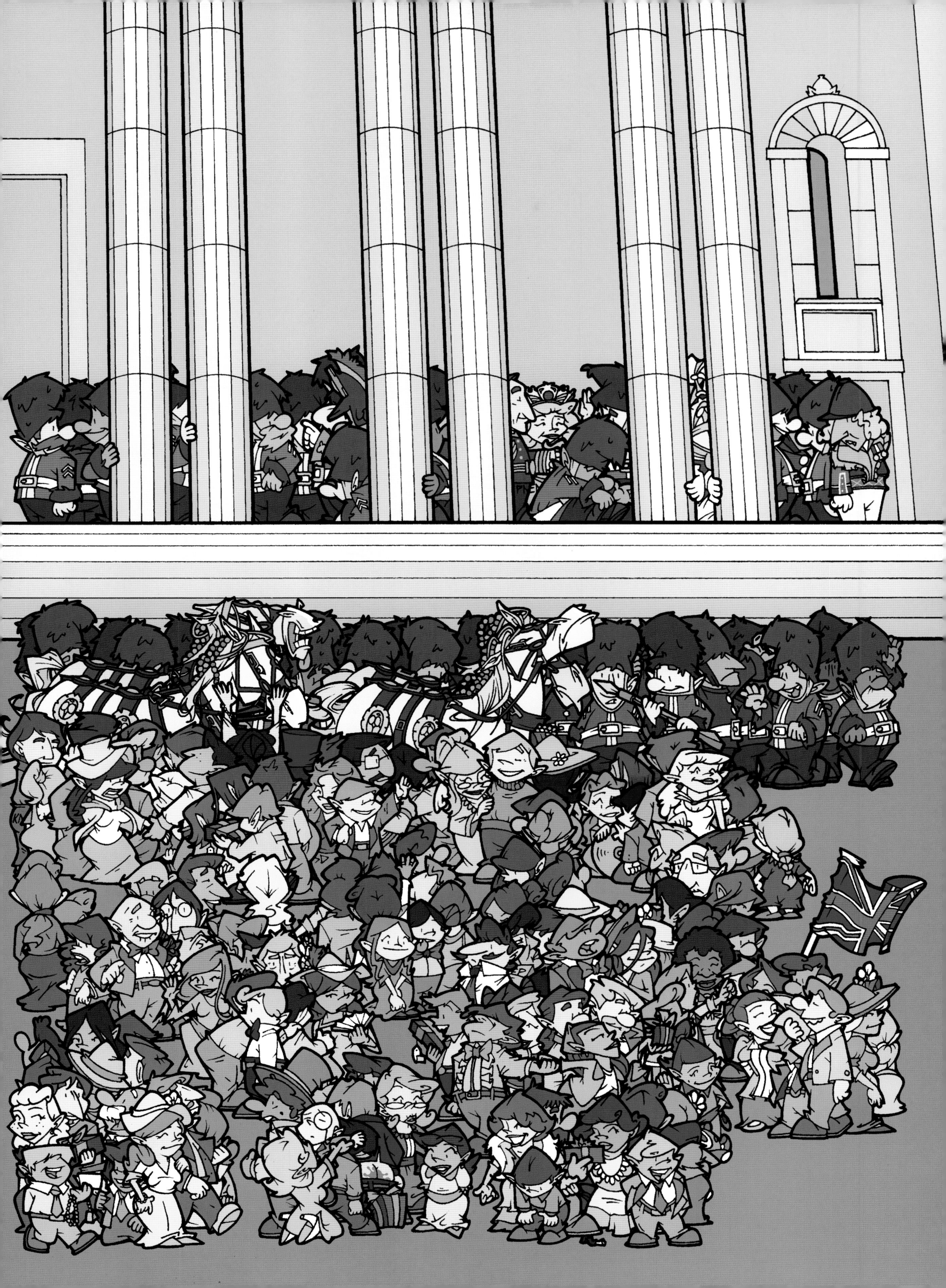

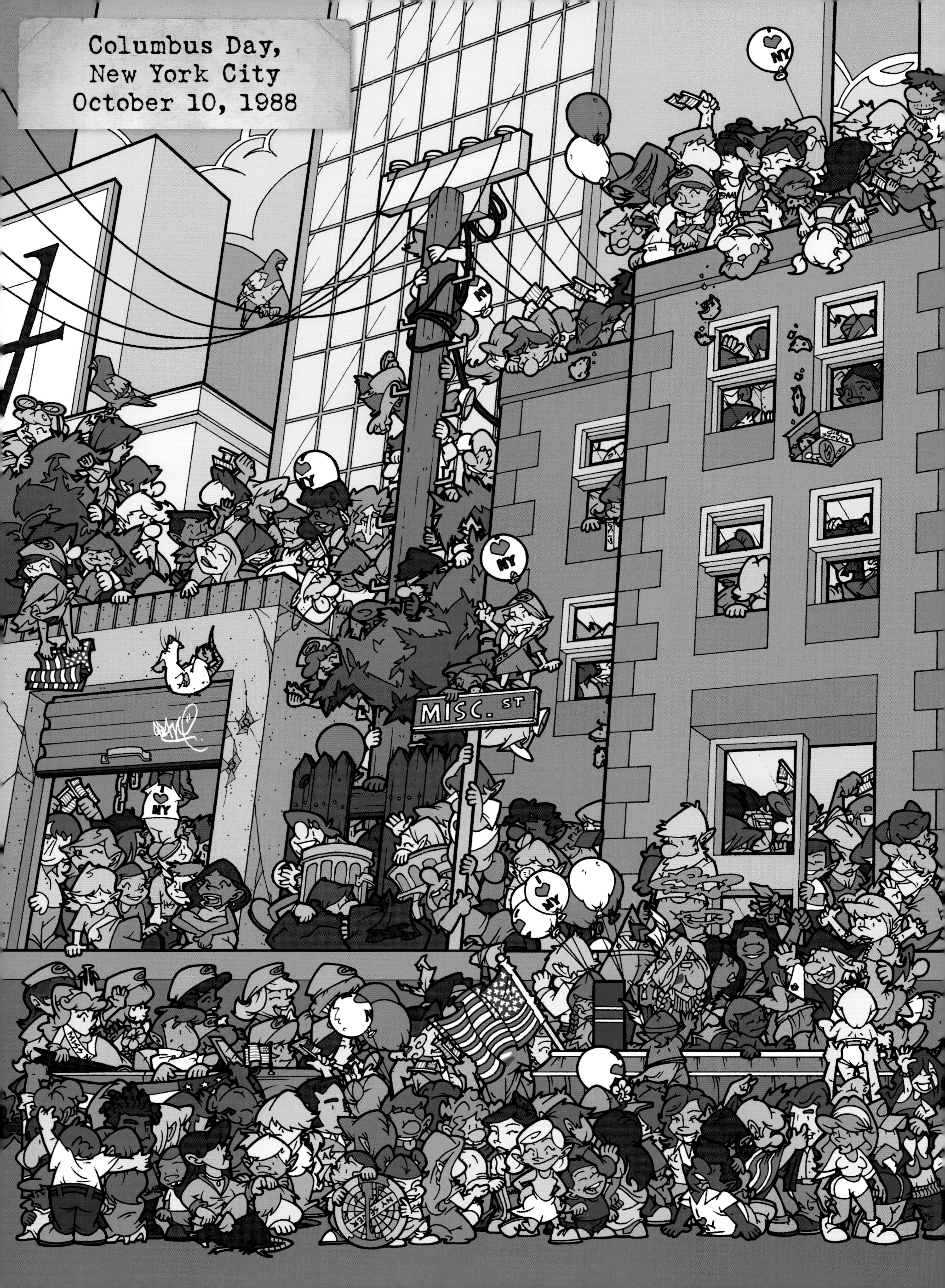
Columbus Day,
New York City
October 10, 1988
MISC. ST

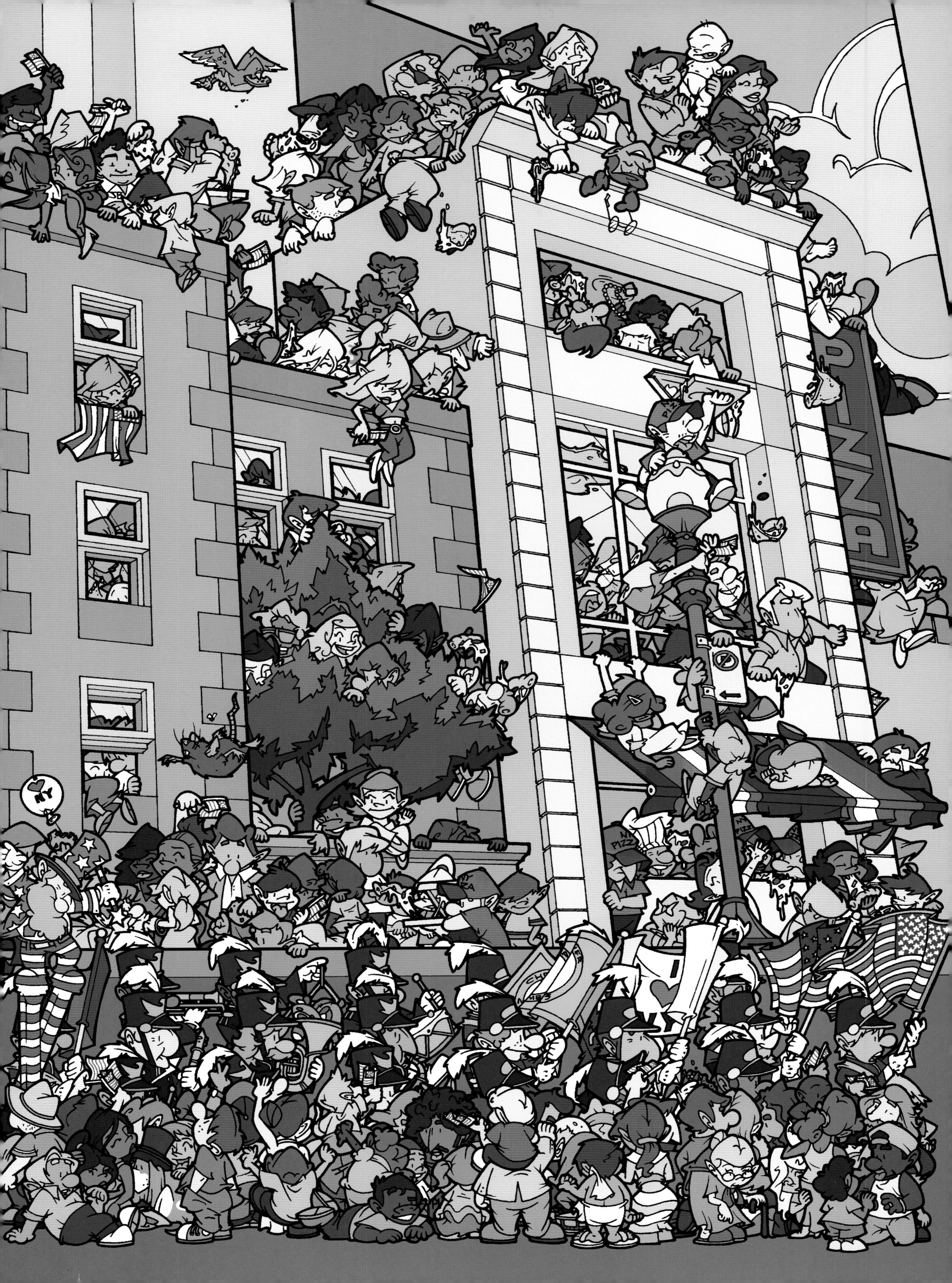
NY

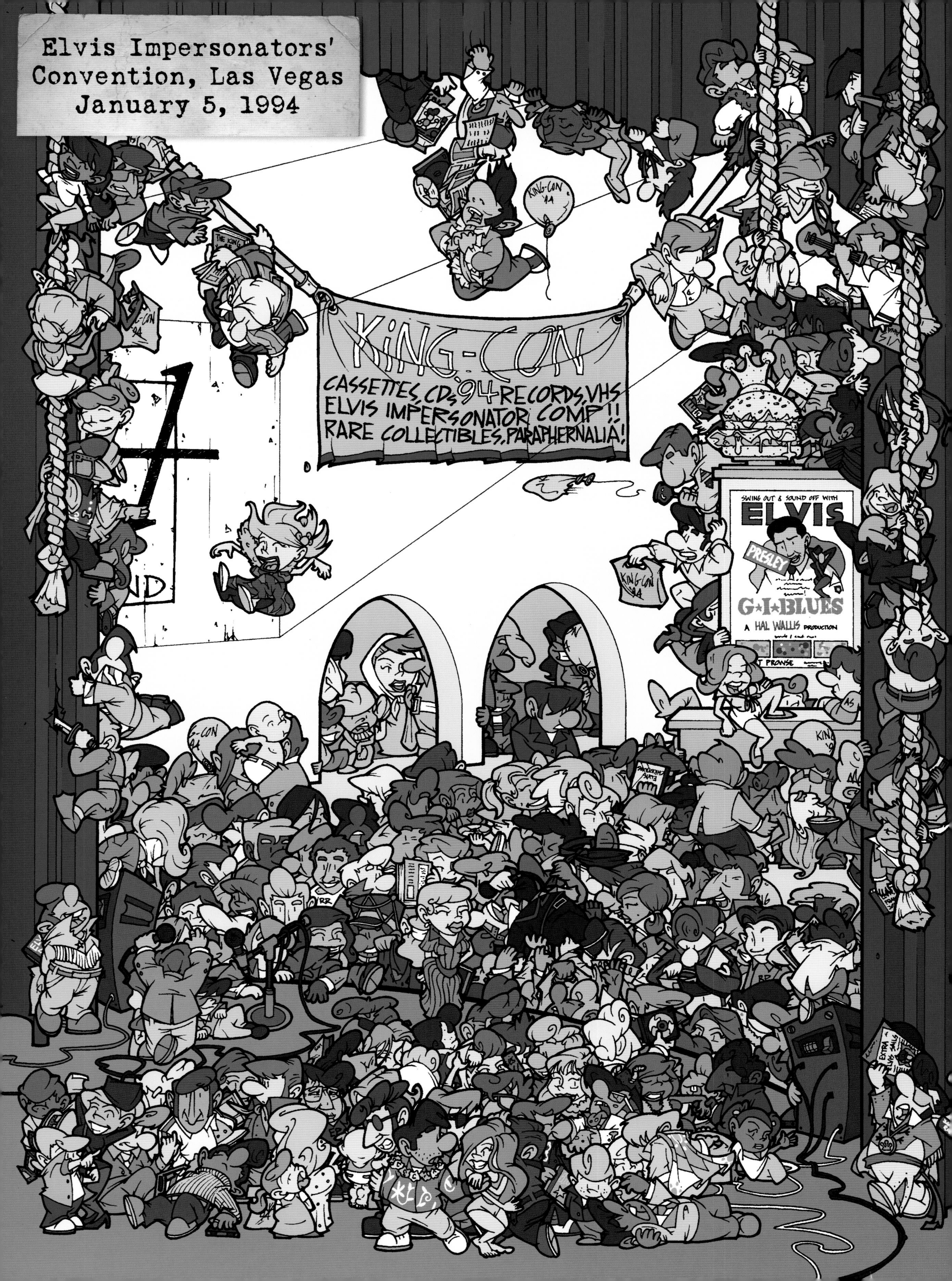
Elvis Impersonators' Convention, Las Vegas January 5, 1994
KiNG-CON
CASSETTES, CDs '94 RECORDS, VHS
ELVIS IMPERSONATOR COMP!!
RARE COLLECTIBLES, PARAPHERNALIA!
KING-CON '94
SWING OUT & SOUND OFF WITH
ELVIS
PRESLEY
G·I·BLUES
A HAL WALLIS PRODUCTION

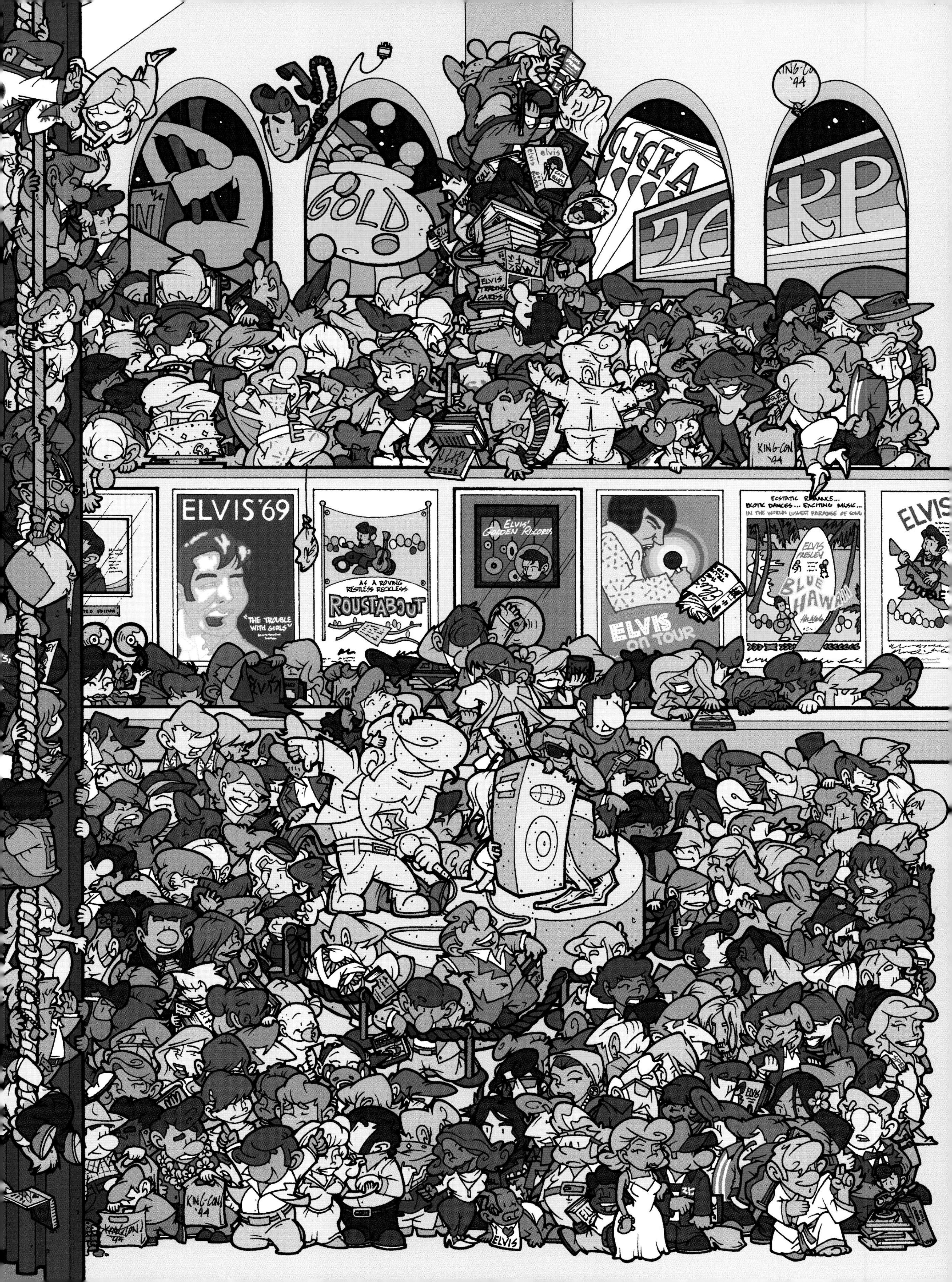

GOLD
KING-CON '94
ELVIS TRADING CARDS
ELVIS '69
"THE TROUBLE WITH GIRLS"
AS A ROVING RESTLESS RECKLESS
ROUSTABOUT
ELVIS' GOLDEN RECORDS
ELVIS ON TOUR
ECSTATIC ROMANCE... EXOTIC DANCES... EXCITING MUSIC...
IN THE WORLDS LUSHEST PARADISE OF SONG
ELVIS PRESLEY
BLUE HAWAII
ELVIS
DOUBLE
KING-CON '94
KING-CON '94
I ♥ ELVIS

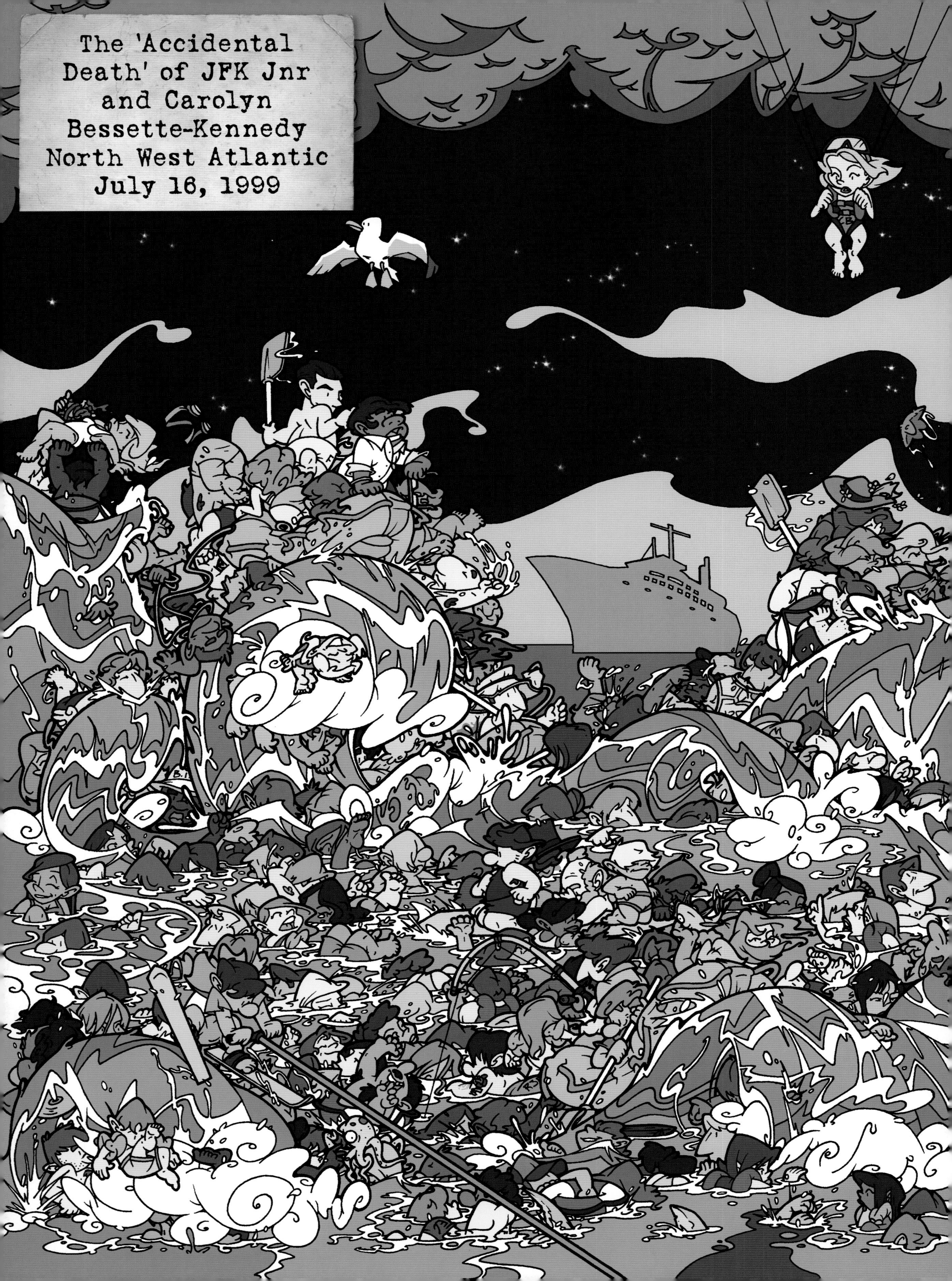
The 'Accidental Death' of JFK Jnr and Carolyn Bessette-Kennedy North West Atlantic July 16, 1999

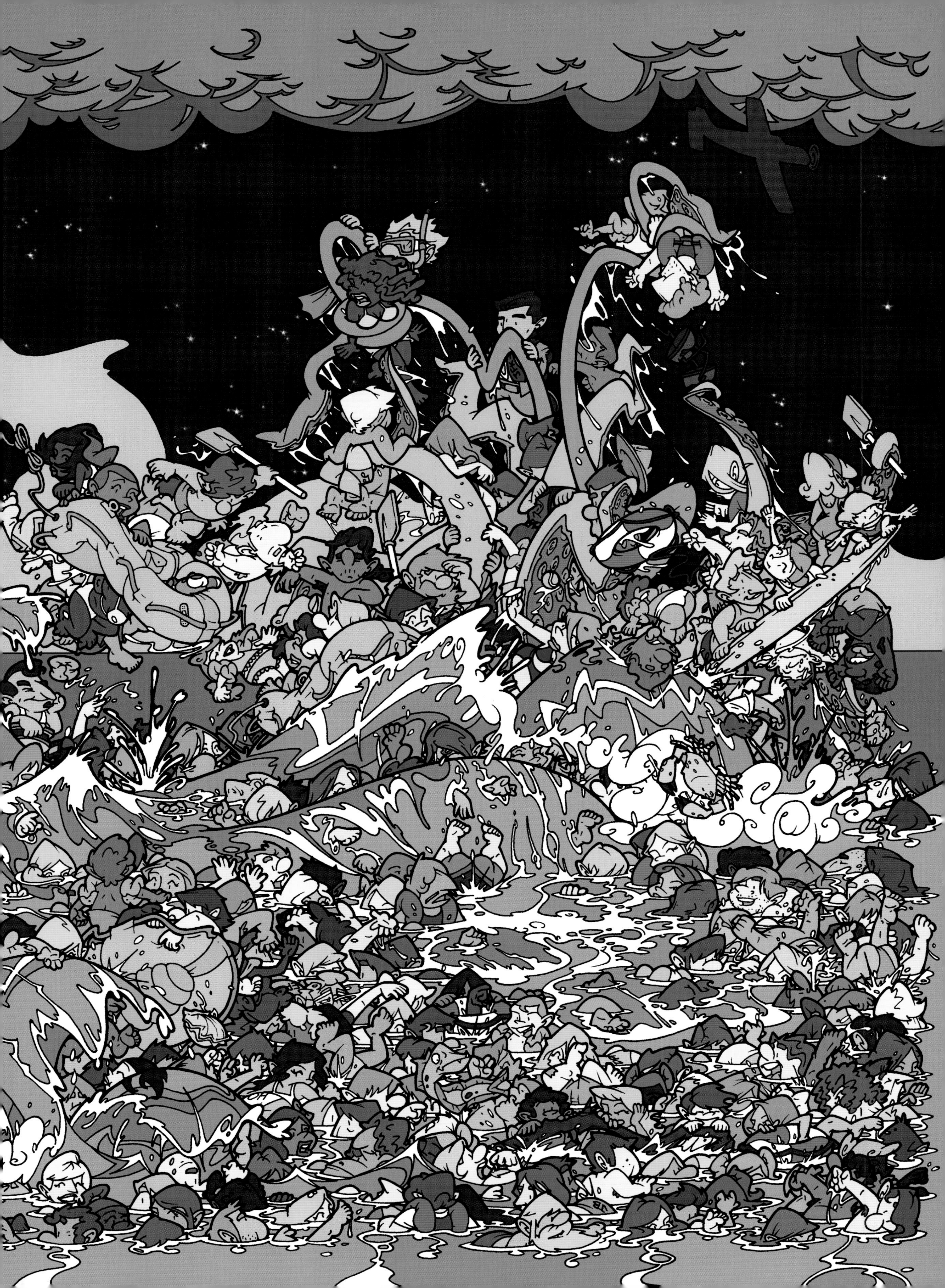

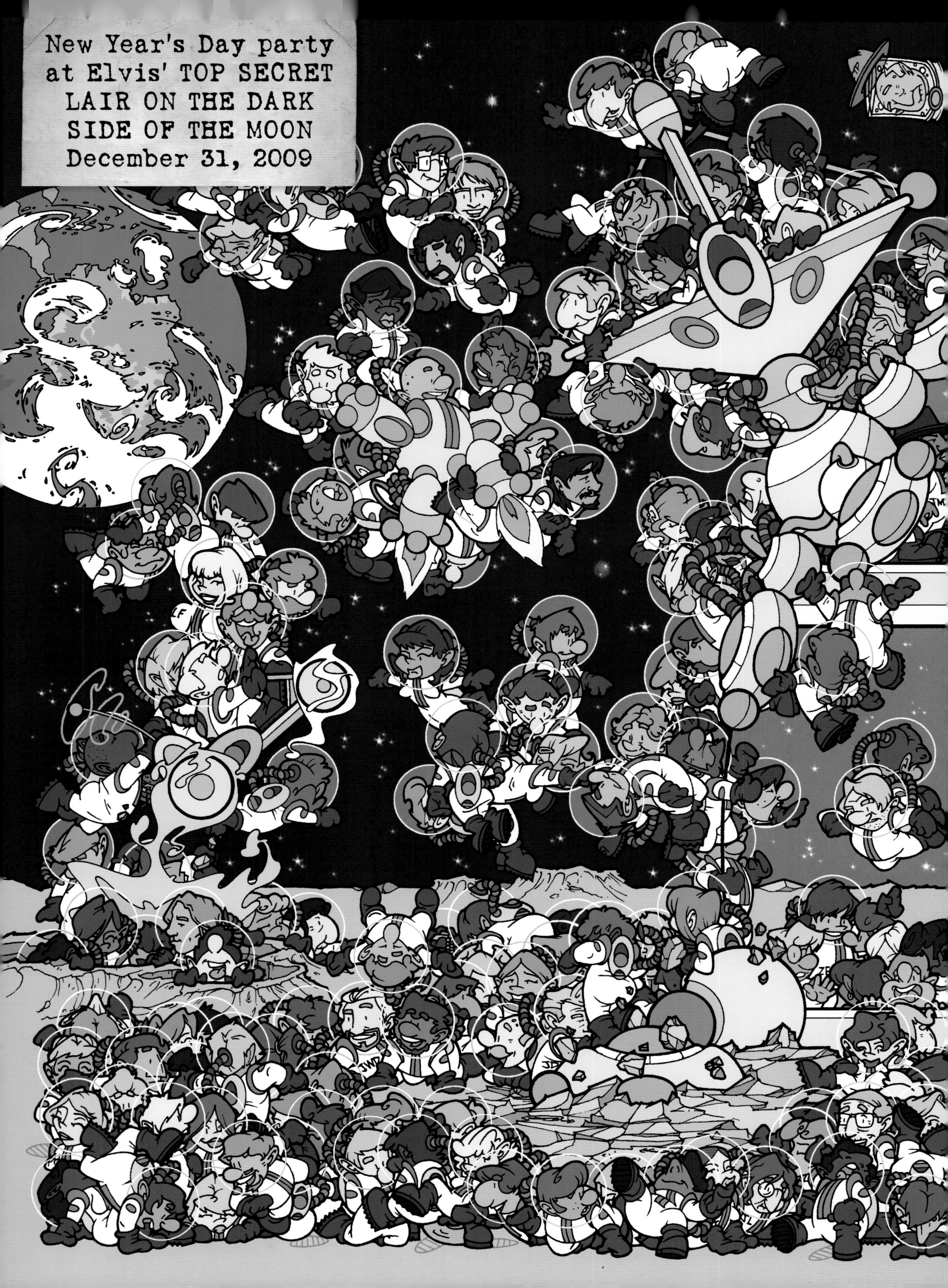
New Year's Day party
at Elvis' TOP SECRET
LAIR ON THE DARK
SIDE OF THE MOON
December 31, 2009

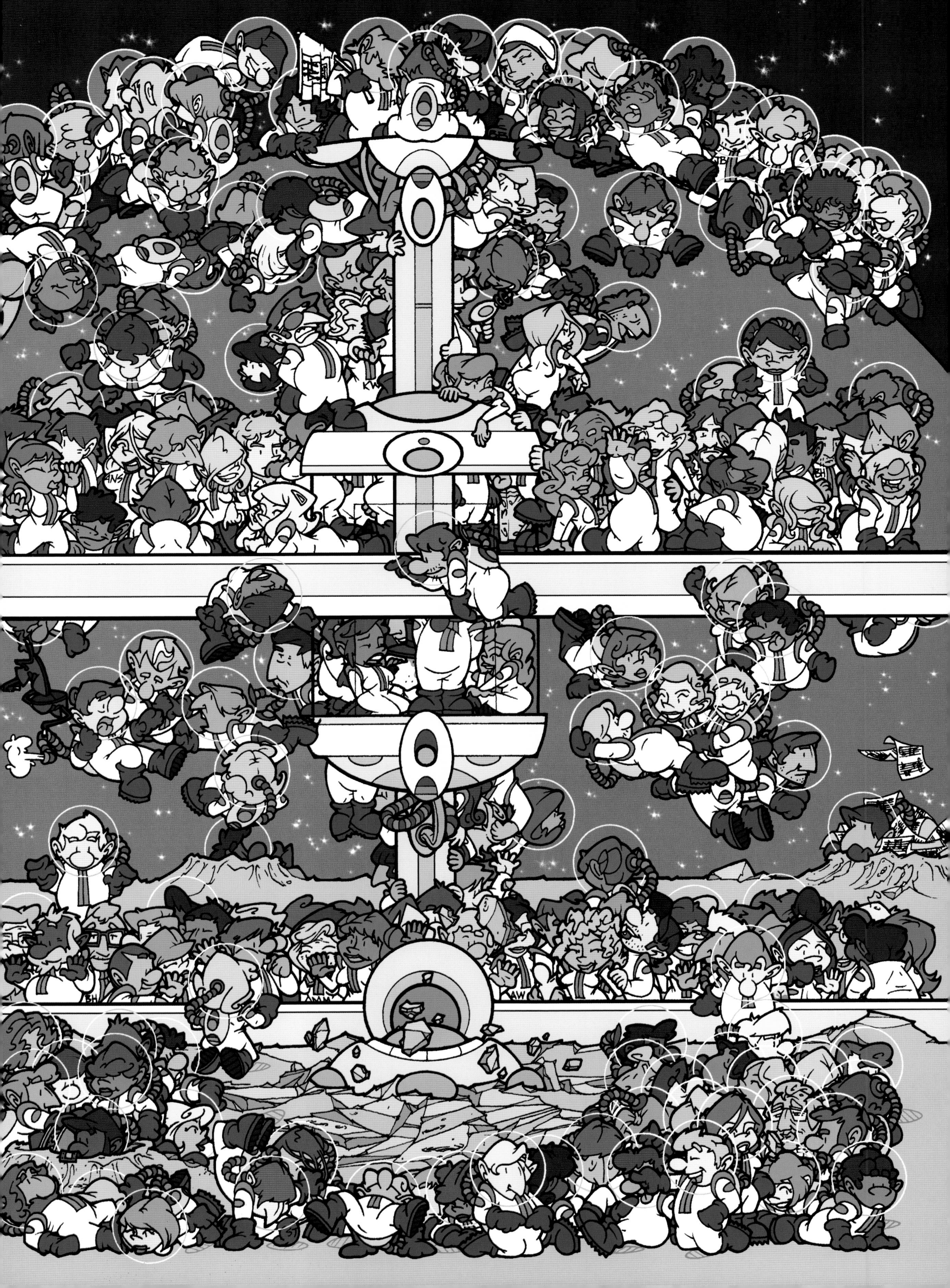

Checklists and Notes for the Eager Investigator
FURTHER THINGS AND PEOPLE TO LOOK FOR

Note: The '†' sign next to the celebrity's name indicates that the person in question was supposedly dead at the time that the photo was taken.

Panel 1 – 'Jailhouse Rock' Cast Wrap Up Party, July 1, 1957.
- [ ] Elvis
- [ ] James Dean (1931 – 1955) †
- [ ] Eva Peron (1919 – 1952) †
You can hardly see her face in this one but I suspect that Eva was the one who first faked her death five years earlier so that she could live off her Swiss bank accounts. I also theorize that Elvis used Charlie and James as his first 'practice runs'. His co-star in jailhouse rock, Judy Tyler 'died' a few days after the photo was taken. Maybe she was practice too …
- [ ] Director Richard Thorpe
- [ ] Co-star Judy Tyler who plays Peggy Van Alden (1933 – 1957)
- [ ] Mickey Shaughnessy who plays Hunk Houghton
- [ ] Seven gold musical instruments

Panel 2 – The Day the Music 'Died', Field in Clear Lake, Iowa, February 3, 1959
Here we have the crowded crash site of the downed plane that 'killed':
- [ ] Buddy Holly (1936 – 1959) †
- [ ] Ritchie Valens (1941 – 1959) †
- [ ] Jiles Perry 'The Big Bopper' Richardson (1930 – 1959) †
- [ ] Dead pilot Rodger Peterson
Also look for:
- [ ] Elvis
- [ ] 'Winter Dance Party Tour' flyers x3
- [ ] Thermomter 18°F
- [ ] Valens 50c coin
- [ ] Making a snow angel
- [ ] 'Bob' writing his name in the snow
- [ ] Dwyer Flying Service ticket (singed)
- [ ] Holly's Gun
- [ ] And there's this sad-looking kid who looks to be around 13-years-old and who looks a hell of a lot like a young Don MacLean holding an apple pie.

Panel 3 – The 'Death' of Marilyn Monroe, Brentwood, California, August 5, 1962
- [ ] Elvis
- [ ] Marilyn Monroe (1926 – 1962) †
- [ ] Mario Lanza (1921 – 1959) †
- [ ] Eddie Cochran (1938 – 1960) †
- [ ] Stuart Sutcliffe – The original bassist with The Beatles (1940 – 1962) † has a beetle crawling on him.
- [ ] Ernest Hemmingway (1899 – 1961) †
- [ ] John Fitzgerald Kennedy (1917 – 1963)
- [ ] Bobby Kennedy (1925 – 1968)
- [ ] Joe DiMaggio – with a baseball bat
- [ ] Arthur Miller
- [ ] Eunice Murray (Marilyn's maid)
- [ ] Jack Clemmons and Pat Newcombe (Officers of the LAPD)
- [ ] Dr Ralph Greenson (Marilyn' psychiatrist)
- [ ] Frank Sinatra
- [ ] Dean Martin – with a bottle of booze
- [ ] Sammy Davis Jnr
- [ ] Peter Lawford – smoking a cigarette
- [ ] Joey Bishop
- [ ] Judy Garland (1922 – 1969) – with a palm full of pills
- [ ] December 1953 copy of Playboy

- [ ] Telephone
- [ ] Candles x 7
- [ ] Bottle of 'Nembutal' pills

Panel 4 – On the set of the film 'Paradise Hawaiian Style', August 18, 1965
- [ ] Elvis
- [ ] Patsy Cline (1932 – 1963) †
- [ ] Sam Cooke (1922 – 1964) †
- [ ] JFK (1917 – 1963) †
- [ ] Sylvia Plath (1932 – 1963) †
- [ ] Malcolm X (1925 – 1965) †
- [ ] Tom Parker (1909 – '1997')
- [ ] Helicopter key lost in the sand
- [ ] Co-star Suzanna Leigh who plays Judy Hudson
- [ ] James Shigeta who plays Danny Kohana
- [ ] Donna Butterworth who plays Jan Kohana
- [ ] Paradise Hawaiian Style movie poster
- [ ] Director Michael D. Moore

Panel 5 – A racing scene on the set of the film 'Speedway', July 20, 1967
- [ ] Elvis
- [ ] Jayne Mansfield (1933 – 1967) †
- [ ] Brian Epstein (1934 – 1967)
- [ ] Yuri Gagarin (1934 – 1968)
- [ ] Che 'It worked for Malcolm' Guevara (1928 – 1967)
- [ ] Martin Luther 'It worked for Malcolm and Che' King Jnr (1929 – 1968)
- [ ] Joe Orton (1933 – 1967)
- [ ] Otis Redding (1941 – 1967)
- [ ] Tom Parker (1909 – '1997')
- [ ] Pricilla Presley pregnant, has morning sickness
- [ ] Co-star Nancy Sinatra who plays Susan Jacks
- [ ] Bill Bixby who plays Kenny Donford
- [ ] Director Norman Taurog
- [ ] Miss Charlotte Speedway 100
- [ ] Go Go to Go doggy bags from the 'Drive In A Go Go' restaurant x 3

Panel 6 – Party at an undisclosed location, September 28, 1974
- [ ] Elvis
- [ ] Sharon Tate (1946 – 1969) †
- [ ] Brian Jones (1942 – 1969) †
- [ ] Jimi Hendrix (1942 – 1970) †
- [ ] Janis Joplin (1943 – 1970) †
- [ ] Yukio Mishima (1925 – 1970) †
- [ ] Duane Allman (1946 – 1971) †
- [ ] Jim Morrison (1943 – 1971) †
- [ ] Edie Sedgwick (1943 – 1971) †
- [ ] Pier Angeli (1932 – 1971) †
- [ ] Jim Croce (1943 – 1973) †
- [ ] Bobby Darin (1936 – 1973) †
- [ ] Paul Williams (1939 – 1973) †
- [ ] Bruce Lee (1940 – 1973) †
- [ ] Literature titled 'Hippie Hygiene'
- [ ] Nosebleed
- [ ] Overdose victim frothing at the mouth

Panel 7 – The 'Funeral' and Vigil at Graceland, August 18, 1977

Note: 30 fans attended the ceremony, Sammy. If only they knew!

- ❑ Elvis
- ❑ Cass Elliot (1941 – 1974) † eating a huge submarine ham sandwich
- ❑ Tim Buckley (1947 – 1975) †
- ❑ Anissa Jones (1958 – 1976) †
- ❑ Sal Mineo (1939 – 1976) †
- ❑ Freddie Prinze (1954 – 1977) †
- ❑ Marc Bolan (1947 – 1977) †
- ❑ Steve 'It worked for Che, Malcolm and Martin' Biko (1946 – 1977)
- ❑ Priscilla Presley
- ❑ Lisa Marie Presley
- ❑ Vernon Presley (1916 – 1979)
- ❑ Tom Parker (1909 – '1997') wearing a Hawaiian shirt and shorts (this actually happened!!!)
- ❑ James Brown
- ❑ George Hamilton – heavily tanned
- ❑ Jackie Kahane
- ❑ 'Dearly Missed' New Holland greeting card
- ❑ A particularly snotty handkerchief

Panel 8 – The Royal Wedding, St. Paul's Cathedral, London, July 29, 1981

This photo is proof positive that Elvis knows how to think long-term!!!

- ❑ Elvis
- ❑ Sandy Denny (1947 – 1978) †
- ❑ Keith Moon (1946 – 1978) †
- ❑ Nancy Spudgen (1958 – 1978) †
- ❑ Sid Vicious (1957 – 1979) †
- ❑ Minnie Ripperton (1947 – 1979) †
- ❑ John Bonham (1948 – 1980) †
- ❑ Bon Scott (1946 – 1980) †
- ❑ John Lennon (1940 – 1980) †
- ❑ Bob Marley (1945 – 1981) †
- ❑ Chuck and Di
- ❑ Liz and Phil
- ❑ Camilla Parker Bowles (as she was at the time)
- ❑ A wedding gift with colours of wrapping reversed
- ❑ Horse performing a bowel movement

Panel 9 – Columbus Day, New York City, October 10, 1988

- ❑ Elvis
- ❑ John Belushi (1949 – 1982) †
- ❑ Karen Carpenter (1950 – 1983) †
- ❑ Denis Wilson (1944 – 1983) †
- ❑ Andy Kaufman (1949 – 1984) †
- ❑ Barbara Yung Mei Ling (1959 – 1985) †
- ❑ Masako Natsume (1957 - 1985) †
- ❑ Gia Carangi (1960 – 1986) †
- ❑ Phil Lynott (1949 – 1986) †
- ❑ Hillel Slovak (1962 – 1988) †
- ❑ Jean-Michel Basquiat (1960 – 1988) †
- ❑ Andy Gibb (1958 – 1988) †
- ❑ New York City rats x 3
- ❑ Pigeon stealing away a Girl Scout cookie

Panel 10 – Elvis Impersonators' Convention, Las Vegas, January 5, 1994

- ❑ Elvis
- ❑ Stevie Ray Vaughn (1954 – 1990) †
- ❑ Steve Clark (1960 – 1991) †
- ❑ Karen Young (1951 – 1991) †
- ❑ Yutaka Ozaki (1965 – 1992) †
- ❑ Sam Kinison (1953 – 1992) †
- ❑ Brandon 'It worked for Dad' Lee (1965 - 1993) †
- ❑ Kurt Cobain (1967 – 1994)
- ❑ Andreas Escobar (1967 – 1994)
- ❑ River Phoenix (1970 – 1993) †
- ❑ Roland Ratzenberger (1960 – 1994)
- ❑ Ayrton Senna (1960 – 1994)
- ❑ Wobble/Bobble head Elvis statue
- ❑ Elvis comic book, issue one
- ❑ 'The King' Figurine MOC (Mint On Card)
- ❑ A lock of Elvis' hair

Panel 11 – The 'Accidental Death' of JFK Jnr and Carolyn Bessette-Kennedy – North West Atlantic, July 16, 1999

- ❑ Elvis
- ❑ JFK Jr (1960 – 1999) and Carolyn Bessette-Kennedy (1966 – 1999) †
- ❑ Falco (1957 – 1998) † calling Vienna from a payphone
- ❑ Selena (1971 – 1995) †
- ❑ Richey James Edwards (1967 – 1995?) †
- ❑ Ingo Schwichtenberg (1965 – 1995) †
- ❑ Tupac Shakur 1971 – 1996) †
- ❑ Eva Cassidy (1963 – 1996) †
- ❑ Notorious B.I.G. (1972 – 1997) †
- ❑ Jeff 'It worked for my Dad too' Buckley (1966 – 1997) †
- ❑ Chris Farley (1964 – 1997) †
- ❑ Michael Hutchence (1960 – 1997) †
- ❑ Dana Plato (1964 – 1999) †
- ❑ Ofra Haza (1957 – 2000)
- ❑ Fish with hook still in mouth

Panel 12 – New Year's Day party at Elvis' TOP SECRET LAIR ON THE DARK SIDE OF THE MOON, December 31, 2009

I think my informant must have gotten this by satellite!!!

- ❑ Elvis
- ❑ Lolo Ferrari (1962 - 2000) †
- ❑ Aaliyah (1979 – 2001) †
- ❑ Kim Walker (1968 – 2001) †
- ❑ Chuck Shuldiner (1967 – 2001) †
- ❑ Ben Hollioake (1977 – 2002) †
- ❑ Layne Staley (1967 – 2002) †
- ❑ Jam Master J (1965 – 2002) †
- ❑ Jonathan 'It worked for River' Brandis (1976 – 2003) †
- ❑ Dimebag Darrell (1966 – 2004) †
- ❑ Eddie Guerrero (1967 – 2005) †
- ❑ Steve Irwin (1962 – 2006) †
- ❑ Jan Werner Danielsen (1976 – 2006) †
- ❑ Anna Nicole Smith (1967 – 2007) †
- ❑ Dan Fogelberg (1951 – 2007) †
- ❑ Benazir 'It worked for Malcolm, Martin and Steve' Bhutto (1956 – 2007) †
- ❑ Suzanne Tamim (1977 – 2008) †
- ❑ Heath Ledger (1979 – 2008) †
- ❑ Tom Cruise
- ❑ Paris Hilton
- ❑ Amy Whinehouse
- ❑ Zach Efron
- ❑ Ashley Olsen
- ❑ A futuristic ray gun

And check out the older versions of:
- ❑ James Dean
- ❑ Marilyn Monroe
- ❑ John Lennon
- ❑ Buddy Holly
- ❑ Tom Parker's (1909 – 1997) head in a jar

First published in 2009 by
New Holland Publishers Pty Ltd
Sydney · Auckland · London · Cape Town

1/66 Gibbes Street Chatswood NSW 2067 Australia
218 Lake Road Northcote Auckland New Zealand
86 Edgware Road London W2 2EA United Kingdom
80 McKenzie Street Cape Town 8001 South Africa

A record of this book is held at the National Library of Australia

ISBN 9781741107029

Managing Director and Publisher: Fiona Schultz – Shoe Size 8 – Burning Love
Financial Director: Phillip Shaw – Shoe Size – 7½ – Suspicious Minds
Publishing Manager: Lliane Clarke – Shoe Size 6 – You Were Always On My Mind
Production Manager: Olga Dementiev – Shoe Size 7½ – Can't Help Falling In Love With You
Publicity Manager: Ian Dodd – Shoe Size 10 – Girls Girls Girls
Digital Manager: Warren Moore – Shoe Size 7 Maybe 6 – American Trilogy
National Accounts Manager: Julianne Woolfe – Shoe Size 6 – Blue Hawaii
Sales Manager: Jackie Wilson – Shoe Size 6 – In The Ghetto
Accountant: Mark Andrews – Shoe Size 9 or 10 – Jailhouse Rock
Commissioning Editor: Diane Jardine – Shoe Size 7½ – A Little Less Conversation
Accounts Manager: Tony Dunne – Shoe Size 8½ – Blue Suede Shoes
Product Manager: Lesley Pagett – Shoe Size 10 – Love Me Tender
Designer On This Book: Hayley Norman – Shoe Size 9 – Hound Dog
Sales Co-ordinator: Triny O'Sullivan – Shoe Size 7½ – Mamma Liked The Roses
Designer: Tania Gomes – Shoe Size 7 – Viva Las Vegas
Publishing Executive: Diane Ward – All Shook Up
Receptionist: Ishbel Thorpe – Shoe size 6½ – A Thing Called Love
Junior Editor: Ashlea Wallington – Summer Kisses, Winter Tears

Printer: Tien Wah Press (Malaysia) Pty Ltd

10 9 8 7 6 5 4 3 2 1

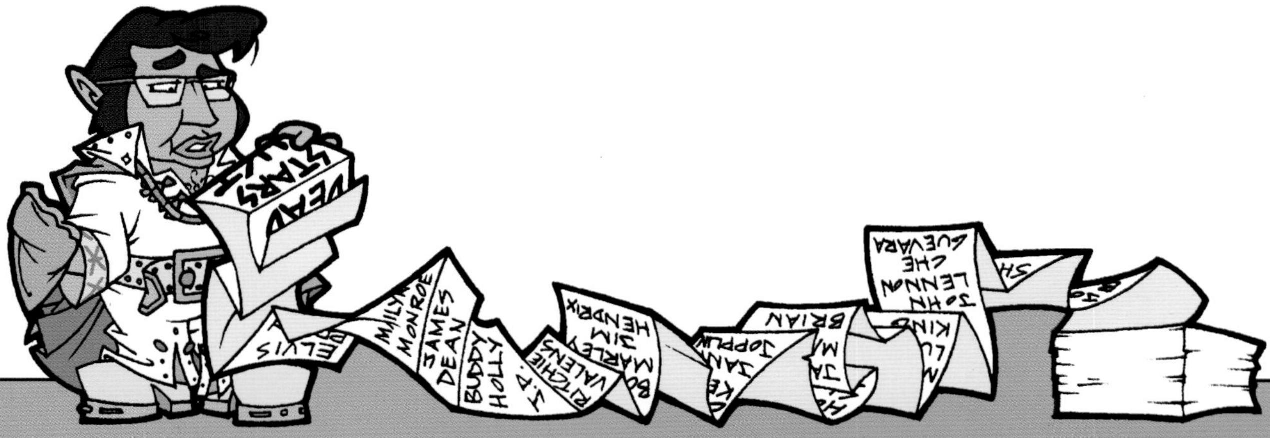
ELVIS
JAMES DEAN
BUDDY HOLLY
JOHN LENNON
CHE GUEVARA